50/50

Finding Life's Balance for All Human Beings

GREGORY L. DOCTOR

Published in the United States of America

Brilliant Books Literary
137 Forest Park Lane Thomasville
North Carolina 27360 USA

ISBN:
Paperback: 979-8-88945-399-4
Ebook: 979-8-88945-400-7
Hardback: 979-8-88945-401-4

CONTENTS

INTRODUCTION

I would like to start out this book by providing some background about myself. I was born the youngest of four biological children in Charleston, South Carolina, having two older brothers, Herman Myron Doctor and Kerman Duvall Doctor, and a sister, Pamela Renee Doctor. When I was fourteen years old, my mother and my father adopted my little sister, Laquana, to fulfill my older sister's wishes of having a younger sister. She was a handicapped "Wednesday's child" who had been featured on a weekly show that the local television stations broadcasted in the indigenous area of Charleston, South Carolina.

We were brought up under strict guidance from our parents, Herman and Vermell Doctor, and Strong Grand Parents. We were blessed to be raised we both parental figures and a bonus village throughout our childhood. They understood the struggles that most minorities must go through in order to be successful. They instilled in us respect for God, self, and people, regardless of the color of their skin or the deficiency of their character, but also taught us to always demand the reciprocal. Growing up as the youngest, I was afforded the opportunity to observe many good decisions, as well as bad decisions, made by my older siblings. This helped strengthen me more as a young black man trying to succeed in a very rigid world. At a very early age, back in 1975, I was intertwined with my best friend, William Gilliard—known then as Tony and now as Dr. Gilliard—as bus 51 picked him up from the bus stop two minutes from my home. He and I started a journey that we still travel to this very day (more on a mental level now). We set goals and challenged ourselves to reach beyond our preconceived limitations. We set the bar so high that if we did not achieve our goals, at least by getting close to the goal we would still be successful. This state of mind propelled us in sports and many other areas of life as young teenagers. We were both blessed to have strong father figures while growing up. I can truly attribute who I am today not only to having one strong father but to having had many strong father figures throughout my childhood. They taught us the importance of always keeping God at the head of everything in life.

The old adage "It takes a village to raise a child" was so true and relevant in our small community of Sanders. The one-way-in and one-way-out road that we grew up on was filled with family and friends, and the friends were also family in everyone's eyes. All the families in the Sanders, Ponderosa, and Red Top communities were extremely tight-knit.

Tony and I would take walks and talk about things we wanted to accomplish in life and where we wanted to be by adulthood. Thanks to the love of God, both of us are still healthy and are forging ahead toward the next chapters of our untold stories.

My childhood seemed to be like a heavenly dream. My brothers and I played basketball, football, hunted, built clubhouses, and went fishing with our cousins, Sammy and Reesie, who were also our next-door neighbors. They were more like brothers than cousins. We did everything that kids did growing up in the country with all our other cousins as well (Joe Joe, Darren, Tony, Dwayne "Caveman," Maurice, Ira, Sidney, Willis, Malcolm, Michael and so many others throughout our community). Honestly, there are too many cousins, friends, and family members to list and I apologize to those that know that they are closely apart of my story and are not listed. Our childhood was very much diverse; we were not limited to the south and spent most of our childhood and upbringing between Charleston, S.C., Bronz, NY, and New Jersey. Some of my mother's sisters and brothers remained in New York and most of my father's family lived in New Jersey as well. They both lived in both states and moved back down to Charleston when my mother was pregnant with my eldest brother Myron.

I started noticing a change in my demeanor and my priorities around my junior year in high school. The words, stories, and thoughts set out by older individuals became more important to me. I would go and sit with and listen to my grandfather Legare, who was a preacher, and my grandfather Doctor, who was also heavily involved with the church. My Grand-Uncle Reverend Joseph Heyward (Uncle Bubzie, My Pastor and mentor) and Reverend Robert Deas (Dr. Gilliard's father) from across the tracks— Both men were instrumental in my life, family and the heads of two successful churches in Charleston County. They provided countless tales and insights into a challenging life that I was about to embark on. My dad, along with these men, influenced me in ways that are still unexplainable today. They told me about the old times and how important it is to always have a sense of urgency about the importance of making a difference in this short life that God has granted each of us. Influenced by many successful men, I was determined to be different and to make wise decisions based on respecting others and catapulting myself toward success as an individual of God, as well as to strengthen my psyche, so that one day I could make an impact on this world.

My father would constantly challenge my psyche everyday when would be headed out to construction jobsites. If was very baffling to me at that time but I truly have a clear understanding of what is was doing now. He was making me different and unique, as he constantly told me when I was young. "Greg you are already an unique individual, but you must be different, be different Greg." He saw something in me that I did not see in myself until many decades later. He would ask me, out of nowhere ask, Greg, what is 55x8, Greg what is 203 divided by 9, Greg what is 3/4" minus 3/8"and so on. This was challenging at first, but over time it became easier for me to do head math and to analyze difficult things with ease. He would ask philosophical things that would drive my mind into a critical thinking stage at these early teen years of my life. Looking back in retrospect, he made me different and contributed significantly to the critical thinker I am today. He has been absent out of our lives for more than two decades now, but I just want to thank him for molding me into the man I am today. There is so much I can write about this man, but those that knew him, know that it still would not be enough said about him as a person, his character, and the things he did in the short 50 years of life that God granted him on this earth.

At this time, it was not clear to me how important education was in becoming an accomplished and successful individual in this mundane life. Fortunately, I graduated from high school at the age of seventeen without failing any grades (this was very challenging, but thanks to Mom, it happened). I could write another mini book on why the aforementioned is in parenthesis. Faced with the decision of where to go from there, I contemplated going to college but kept hearing my parents harp about the deficiency of money and how hard it was to make it in this world today. I decided to join the military.

I began the Army's early-entry program in May 1988 and then active service in September 1988. I spent five exciting years in Army Aviation. While I was in, I really embraced education as a true friend, but my immediate duties as a platoon sergeant and crew chief supervisor superseded my educational desires.

After my five years in the military, it was time for me to make another decision as to which direction to go in life. I realized that education was paramount above all besides God and my family. My decision to ETS (expiration of term of service) was a very difficult one because of my love for my military family and the individuals I had met while being in the service. My decision to ETS was based solely on my newly gained clear understanding of me needing more education to excel in this very competitive game we call life.

My life has brought many significant personal, academic, and professional accomplishments that have been very meaningful—from starting out in the military to working on Bell OH-58A, OH-58C, and AH-64A Apache helicopters; to obtaining my FAA civilian aviation mechanics airframe and power plant licenses; to working on all different kinds of civilian airplanes; to obtaining my bachelors of science degrees in both interdisciplinary studies and in aviation, obtaining my master's degree in business law from Regent University's School of Law, to now half way through a Ph.D. in Psychology/Theology at Liberty University.

There are many accomplishments embedded inside of these achievements alone, but as I sit typing and reminiscing on which achievement supersedes the others, one story stands out as a life-learned lesson that needs to be told.

All my experiences in life, coupled with my education, have made me a broader thinker and have brought something to the table for the purpose of conveying a message to the world through this book.

Growing up, our family always gathered for Sunday dinner in the family dining room. We would have our family talk during this time as well. When I was around fourteen years old, at one of these family dinners I was asked by my father, Greg, God bless his soul, "What do you want to be when you grow up?" My retort was that I was going to be a millionaire by the time I was thirty years old. The old man laughed and said, "Why not just say you're going to be financially independent by that age?" I said, "No, I'm going to be a millionaire by the time I am thirty years old."

After this conversation, I charted my life to the best of my young mind's ability to be just what I said I would be. I knew I needed education to accomplish this far-fetched dream of mine. So, while serving my country, I enrolled in correspondence courses and college courses as much as my duties would allow. I realized that concentrating on educating myself was preeminent to achieving being "financially independent." This is one of the reasons I pursued degrees after my military service ended. To make a long story short, the age of thirty has come and gone a long time ago, and the old man was dead on. I definitely became "financially independent"—but not quite a millionaire.

After five long years with the 82nd Airborne Division and 101st Screaming Eagles in the US Army Airborne Divisions and being engaged in two wars overseas, I decided to leave the military and enroll in civilian aviation school. I enrolled in Tidewater Technical Aviation Academy in Virginia Beach, Virginia. The first day of class, the instructor told the class of fifteen members that 66 percent of the people present will not make it to graduation and of the remaining, only 5 percent will go on and be successful in attaining their Airframe and Powerplant Licenses and have rewarding careers in aviation. After this statement, I was determined that I would not be a statistic in any of these percentages. At the end of the course, I was one of three graduates and the only one to graduate with honors.

After graduation I realized that money was not the drive for me wanting to be successful. I had just had my first taste of "thorough education," and I liked it. A thirst for knowledge now became my driving force. After this achievement I felt a sense of accomplishment and pride, and I immediately enrolled at Norfolk State University in Norfolk, Virginia.

During my four years at NSU, I was determined to both finish my degree and graduate with honors. Unfortunately, I had to sit out my senior year due to financial shortcomings after my father unexpectedly passed away, but the love for educating myself helped me overcome this plateau.

After Daddy died, things became really hard for me and the family. I delved into any and everything during this dark time in my life in order to make ends meet and get back into school.

I eventually got back into school and completed both my Bachelor of Science degrees in Interdisciplinary studies and in Aviation. The formidable task of trying to graduate was accomplished in one aspect, but I fell short on hitting the mark of graduating with honors; however, my 2.7 GPA signified honors for all who work full-time jobs and are full-time students at the same time. While pursuing my degrees, I worked full-time hanging drywall at night my entire first and second years. And then I worked full-time (ten-hour shifts) for Piedmont Airlines out of Norfolk International Airport through graduation. My initial years doing these two arduous tasks, all at once, reflected in my GPA. But as I became more and more acclimated to the situation, my grades became better. In my latter years in college, I almost accomplished my second goal. I tell you all of this for young and old minds alike to assimilate it and realize that a 2.7, 3.0, or even a 4.0 does not totally reflect a person's aptitude or what he can really accomplish in this short life here on earth.

Persistency, perseverance, self-determination, and believing that there is a way to accomplish anything in life are a person's greatest traits. My ability to graduate from NSU while working, paying bills, and then paying my entire four-year tuition off three months after graduating signifies more richness in knowledge and direction than most millionaires possess. This achievement alone helped to profoundly strengthen both my mind and spirit.

After receiving my degrees, I moved to Roanoke, Virginia, with my new title as production supervisor for Potomac Airlines. At the time, this job seemed like one of the best things to happen to me. My job was to help establish an operating airline from ground zero, which was very difficult for my young mind. But I shined, and I attribute my success to the goals I set and the challenges I faced in my teenage years. This airline became very successful operating under a Federal Aviation Rule 121 certification, but it was forced to fold because of the United Airlines / US Airways merger being denied by the government. Between July and September of 2001, the airline laid off all their employees. I was once again left with troubling times. There is an old saying that a man's true character and strength will show when he is at his lowest point in life. After this chapter of my life, I was faced with unexpected adversities. I learned how important it is when faced with struggles to remember to look to the heavens—where all blessings come from—keep your faith stronger than ever and allow your adversities to eventually transform into successes. This process will always happen if one has unwavering faith in God and has faith in what exactly you want to accomplish in life.

Right at this same time, 9/11 happened. I was building a garage with an old friend of mine, Ed Meyer. He had worked with me at Potomac Airline in Roanoke, but he left prior to the airline shutting down. While Ed and I were laying out the foundation of the garage, we both received calls, almost simultaneously, with the news that America was under attack. We immediately shut down everything and left to go home to our families.

After this event, I felt compelled to reenlist to bring my experience and knowledge to newer soldiers, so I went back in the Army National Guard, but this time as an officer. I could have done my training in Virginia but I decided to do it in Puerto Rico, because I had recently been studying Spanish in college and wanted to utilize my new skill.

My friend Jesus Ortiz, from US Airways, had helped me with my Spanish and practiced with me nightly at work. I felt confident that I would not have any problems conversing with the indigenous people of Puerto Rico. What I forgot—or at least did not understand— was that this was actual military training and one had to understand, digest, and then divulge the correct information back to the instructors and correctly on tests. Through all of this, God allowed me to become commissioned as an officer and subsequently impart my knowledge on to newer soldiers. Eventually, though, my driving force for educating myself, uninterrupted, forced me to move back into the civilian sector.

This short introduction does not contain all of my achievements, but I felt compelled to allow the reader of this book to also feel some sort of connection with me prior to reading, what I believe, is some life-changing information.

Now let's get into this book, where I try to commingle secular thought with religious thought in order to convey a rich knowledge of us as human beings getting back on the right path of coexisting and loving one another regardless of the color of our skin. This is a subject that has been placed on my heart from God for a while, and I pray that you will be open to this information I have to bring to you.

Finally, I would like to thank my father, Herman Doctor—may he continue to rest in peace—who continuously challenged my mind as a young teenager and instilled greatness in me at an early age. I would also like to thank and dedicate this book to my mother, Vermell Doctor, who has always supported me in everything I've done in life. Immediately after I said several years ago that I was writing a book, she smiled and said, "If you write it, Greg, it will be a best seller." Love you, Momma, and I pray that you stay with us for many more decades to see God's plan for what your son is trying to accomplish in this life. Lastly, I would like to thank my older brother Kerman Doctor for his unconditional love for all his younger brothers and sisters. He stepped in as a father figure to our immediate family after Dad died and does not get the accolades that he has truly earned over the past several decades. Thanks Bro, I love you dearly. To my sisters Pamela Doctor and Laquanna Doctor, I love you both dearly and appreciate your unwavering support and love you have constantly shown me over my entire life. You all are loved dearly.

CHAPTER 1

Being Human

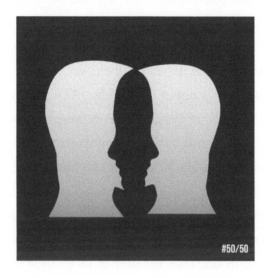

#50/50

Being human—what does that exactly mean? Or better yet, what value does it represent? In the twenty-first century, we must stop and ask ourselves what it actually means to be human. Is it the ability to be rational, as according to some scholars? Or is it that we are the only creatures from God's creation that bury and memorialize our dead?

If we really understand what it is to be human, why isn't this knowledge inherently transparent among all human beings? Yes, this can be taught, but my concern is why isn't it innately ingrained in the hearts of *all* men? Please stop right now and take the time to think about this question in relation to our twenty-first-century problems of racism, the unjustified killing of black men, as well as the inequality among human beings in all societies.

Racism and inequality are not innately human; they are tools of God's fallen angel, the devil. The devil uses these tools to create division within the human race. He has caused a divide from the beginning of time and will continue to cause division until the end of times.

Black men are being killed for sport and subsequently celebrated in private arenas, and then the guilty murderer ends up being exonerated or not indicted by a grand jury. Is this right? Is this of God? And finally, is this a tool of the devil? I will answer all three now. First, it is not right. Secondly, it is not of God by far. And finally, it is definitely a tool of the devil, who is working to continuously divide the human race. If we don't stop, think, evaluate, and fix the problem, then we will definitely lose—not as a black race, but as a human race.

What most people fail to understand is that all the colors of humans are deeply intertwined in this thing called life. If you were to try and exterminate one supposedly called "race" (I say *supposedly* because there is only one race, the human race), then this would be the commencement of exterminating the entire human race.

So here we must be careful. I have placed serious thought and evaluation on this matter. We have an unprecedented number of interracial marriages and mixed children throughout the world. Believe it or not, humans will always fight for their family well before they fight for the color of a person's skin. We must always remember that being human should take precedence above being anything else; everything else is secondary, outside of God.

What one must understand is that the devil must exist in order to bring the best out of us ordinary beings. Without controversy in our lives, we would never be able to enjoy the resilience of successfully overcoming adversity. Humans must understand that through the lens of God we all exist; we do not exist as black humans or white humans. We exist as human beings. Once the order of existence has been learned and accepted by all human beings, then and only then will the eradication of racist ideology begin.

These labels have been placed upon us by the devil in order to establish division. Ever since the devil established the different color labels, he has been able to control peoples' minds, bodies, and souls.

Throughout this book, when I use the term "by the devil," I use it to strictly be associated with God's fallen angel. Unfortunately, some in our society have labeled all white men "blue-eyed devils," even though not all white men participate in the subjugation of others. I am not referring to any group when I speak of the devil; I am strictly talking about the devil himself. To use the term "the devil" and attach it to any group of people would be falling into the same trap that I am trying to prevent others from falling in to.

Unfortunately, it is a reality that the devil has many people who carry his message of evil and wrongdoing throughout the world. His beliefs marinate in their souls. If we want to survive as rationale human beings, we must first give our lives over to the high and mighty and hence eradicate this evil presence off the face of the earth. If the devil is to be eradicated by humans, we must come together and not be separated by races. Only then can we combine our praying voices in order to complete this arduous task. We must start judging one another by our minds and not by the color of someone's skin.

Will this world end due to evil and insidious acts perpetrated by the devil and his followers? I can't answer that question. But I truly believe that, as children of God, we can come together and combat this evil spirit that has progressed uncontrollably throughout our world within the past centuries.

Humans are creative yet at the same time destructive. This is not a bad thing when approaching this particular problem; it is exactly what is needed in order to defeat the devil. We must use our creative side to find a way to unite all humans together to better our world while also using our destructive side to bring down the devil's kingdom. If done simultaneously, this will allow the kingdom of God to eradicate hate, inequality, economic disparity, and racism off the face of the earth. Let us join together as God-fearing people and erase all that divides us and start to live together harmoniously as God wants us to.

The title of this book is *Fifty-Fifty* because everything in our lives is about finding balance. Finding balance between the different demographical groups of people throughout the world, between life and death, between religion and nonreligion, between the rich and the poor, between whites and blacks, and ultimately between good and evil—this is the only way that we will make it as human beings. By finding a sense of balance in life, you will find that life becomes easier to navigate. Without balance, one will always be faced with some sort of controversy.

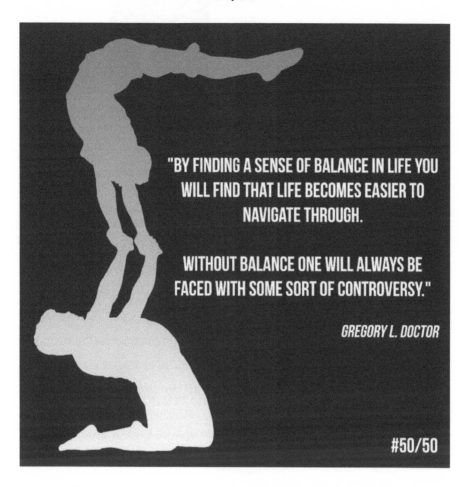

"BY FINDING A SENSE OF BALANCE IN LIFE YOU WILL FIND THAT LIFE BECOMES EASIER TO NAVIGATE THROUGH.

WITHOUT BALANCE ONE WILL ALWAYS BE FACED WITH SOME SORT OF CONTROVERSY."

GREGORY L. DOCTOR

#50/50

I have had to learn about the importance of balance through trial and error throughout most of my adult life. But by keeping an open mind since my early teen years until my present age, I have continuously adjusted in order to be a fifty-fifty human being.

CHAPTER 2

Your Life Is a Lease

As the title says, your life is a lease. We must take heed of this logic, including the significance of these words. God grants man seventy years—that's three scores plus ten on his life's lease. Man's lease may be shortened or man's lease may be extended based upon different variables he encounters in his life. God puts the ball in each individual man's hand; it is your destiny to die, but through discipline to God's word, one can certainly control their timely demise.

Please understand that death is not random. God controls "accidental" death, nonaccidental death, early-age death, and old-age death. There is no such thing as someone dying accidentally; the actual act may have occurred accidentally, but the event that is death was most certainly controlled by God. God gives all human beings the free will to follow his word and teachings or not to follow. The content of his lease to us, as creatures created by him, can be referred to as the Holy Bible.

Since man was created by God and God tells us that the Holy Bible is his word, then the Holy Bible is at the apex of all leases. The words of this lease supersede all other words in any other lease on this planet.

Now, in a lease that has been written by man, there are rules and regulations that every human being must abide by. If the rules are not followed, the tenant can be subjugated to disciplinary actions, up to and including eviction. If man can evict man from a worldly habitat, then God certainly can evict man from his worldly creation, thus being this worldly life that we live.

In God's lease, the rules and regulations are not from this mundane world. It is true that God's lease has rules and regulations as well, but the ramifications of not following his lease—that is "the lease applicable to life," or the Holy Bible—is death.

Death has no number and no announced time when it may happen. The good book tells us that no man knowest the hour, death comes like a thief in the night, and no man is promised tomorrow. If you believe these words and you are a Christian, one has to stop and try to imagine for a moment how God might evaluate your performance according to the rules of his lease. You have to ask yourself, "Right now, will my lease—that is God's lease on my life—be extended or cut short due to my disobedience to the rules and regulations of God's lease?"

As I write these words, I am compelled to let the reader understand that I am just the writer, but I fall prey to my words as well. For Romans 3:23–26 tells us that "we all have sinned and came short of the glory of God." No man is excluded from this statement, and that definitely includes me.

All I am trying to do is carry God's torch in order to strengthen and make clear to believers what God wants and carry his message to nonbelievers, while also passing it on to the youth of this world, so we do not end up in a world permanently filled with abysmal acts. Albeit, we are definitely charting dangerous waters in the world today, as pertaining to evil and abysmal acts. Through persistent teachings that teach righteous words to all humans we can reverse the direction of the world, before it is too late.

Will you play your part in this effort of evil reversal? Or will you be a part of the problem that helps to support the misguided march of human beings of today?

Death is not the only ramification for disobedience to God's rules and regulation of this leased life. God has many answers to disobediences: terminal diseases, physical incapacity, mental incapacity, and so on. He also has many answers to obedience, and these answers are cures to all that I just mentioned.

Some may say that this logic is not accurate, because all of these are tools of the devil. I will not argue that point too much, but what I do understand is that God is the creator of all and holds direct dominion over all things on this earth—and this includes both good and bad events that happen here on earth. If these were solely tools of the devil, then no one could ever be cured; the devil inflicts only bad and never introduces a cure for what he has brought upon a person. Unlike the devil, God does cure, has cured, and continues to cure. So this tells me that both good and bad are tools of God used to strengthen the nonbeliever and to recondition some believers to strengthen their lost faith.

Please understand that the aforementioned diseases are only random examples and should not be looked at subjectively. They have been used solely in order to clarify a point of view.

Everything in our natural world has to follow some sort of system of obedience. Animal life, plant life, and more importantly human life all are embedded within this system. This system is rules and regulations ultimately derived from the most high God. God is everywhere, he see's everything, and he is eternally omnipresence. He is the almighty that terminates and extends leases. I have chosen to walk the straight and narrow in order to have an extended lease on life and to be well learned in Christian life and the afterlife that we call heaven. I also do this in order to exercise all of my God-given talents over a longer period of time here on earth as opposed to having to rush to exercise my talents over a reduced period of time because of disobedience to his word.

What will you choose? Complete disobedience to his lease? Ride both sides of the fence and hope he sympathizes with you and extends your lease? Or will you choose to walk the straight and narrow with him and be guaranteed an extended lease?

Walking with him makes everything else easier in life and allows us to grow to our full potential. Life is already short as it is, so please make the right decision for an extended lease on your life.

CHAPTER 3

Your Death Sentence

Then the LORD God formed a man from the dust of the ground and breathed into his nostrils the breath of life, and the man became a living being.

—Genesis 2:7

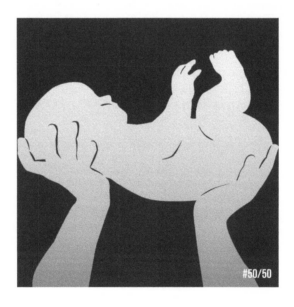

#50/50

When man is born, his life sentence and his death sentence simultaneously begin. In Psalm 90, God tells us that "The days of our years are threescore years and ten; and if by reason of strength they be fourscore years, yet is their strength labor and sorrow; for it is soon cut off, and we fly away." The aforementioned is fascinating to some yet scary to most. Think about how fast the days of our lives are pasting by right now, in this present time, as you read this sentence. I can remember when I was a little boy—not so long ago—playing all types of games and sports with not a worry in the world. Did I think about death at that time? Very rarely I must say. But as we get older and we become wiser, we realize that death is a part of reality. Sure enough, if you are alive you will die, because God tells us that from dust we came and to dust we will return. What a great God; he actually gives us the tools to make our transition to our death sentence more ameliorating. This tool is the word of God from the Bible.

As stated in chapter 2, our life is a lease. Many different variables determine the span of our lease in life. Death surrounds us every moment of our lives and is a commonality that we all share as human beings. This commonality called death resonates mostly with older individuals, yet it is not exclusive to them. God has made death the shadow of life, and it accompanies life at every moment. So the next time you are walking on a bright, sunny day and see your shadow behind you, just remember that this is God telling you that death always accompanies life and that he is with you through both.

Have you ever stopped and thought about just how fragile our lives are? One moment we can be having a great time and enjoying every aspect of our life, and in the blink of an eye our lives can be taken away from us. This fact is not exclusive to the color of one's skin color; it is not exclusive to your position in society, to your bank account, or to anything else in this world. It is only exclusive to all of God's creation, including all animal life, plants, and so on, on this earth. Death is the agent of change. It is the agent that will make any human eradicate hate out of their hearts, even if it is only momentarily.

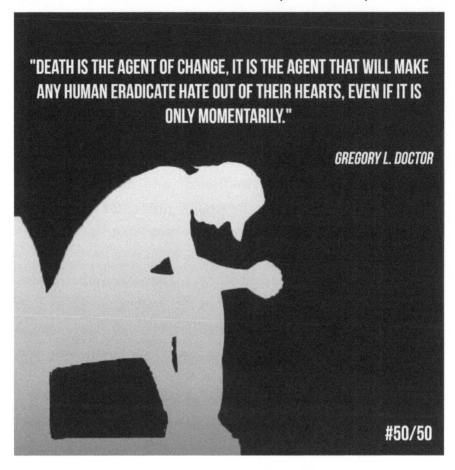

When someone is threatened with death, their entire life's agenda changes as well. This fact tells me that racism is not stamped on anyone's heart; it is a learned behavior that can become "unlearned." This is necessary if we want to erase it off of our earth. Most prejudice individuals have been affected throughout their life by false information that has been fed to them by other prejudice friends and family. This is so unfortunate, especially in our day and time. We are in the twenty-first century of this thing called life, yet we are in the first century of this thing called death when it comes to our mental state.

Life has always been changing since the beginning of time, but death has remained constant. Death stays steady and never changes; it is there morning and night, summer and winter, and with both the young and old.

Throughout our lives, we can all attest to losing someone whom we loved or experiencing unexpected death in some form or another. All of God's creation, both human and animals, have a sense of death. We understand it among our own. Even animals, when visited by death, know that it is the end.

So if we are all God's creation and we all have the commonality of death, why can't we all have the commonality of mutual respect and honor for one another? I will tell you partly why; it is because we have allowed the greed and avariciousness of men in this society to somewhat control our thoughts and, unfortunately, our psyches. If we can stop this controlling factor, then we can overcome the false agenda called racism.

CHAPTER 4

Am I My Brother's Keeper?

As iron sharpens iron one man sharpens another.

—Proverbs 27: 17

This proverb remains relevant in all successful men's lives and should be applied in the daily lives of everyone who strives for a harmonious path toward success. Proverbs 27:17 applies to both men and women. It is a proverb that reaches across all aisles.

In life you must strive to find a challenging supporter who will correct you when you're wrong but also comfort you when comforting is what is needed. In finding that brother or sister who makes you a sharper individual, you can then return the favor and sharpen someone else. We tend to get comfortable with "yes men" being the closest to us, not realizing that we can't grow as much with yes men as we can with individuals who are positively challenging us daily (and I truly stress the word positively).

Throughout your life, take time to ask yourself these questions: "Am I sharpening another brother's life?" or "Is there a brother who is sharpening my life?" If the answer is no to both, then you are not truly living as prosperous of a spiritual life as God has planned for you. You are missing out on knowledge that is gained by embracing influential individuals in your life, and you are ultimately restricting your true growth and potential.

As I have progressed throughout my own life, there have been many men who have truly sharpened me as a person. They have also played a positive role in my constant growth toward finding the answer of why God created me. They have touched my psyche, my physical, and my spiritual being. At the same time, I believe that there are many individuals in this world who will say that Gregory L. Doctor has also sharpened them in one way or another. Life is a gift to all of us from God, and he expects us to positively influence one another so we can grow to our full potential.

Growing to your full potential takes constant effort and constant molding of the mind. Understand that you must choose to embrace the willful gaining of additional knowledge. The molding of the mind has to be conducted by you and reinforced by your brother. This must become a constant daily task if you are expecting greatness in this short time that you have on this earth.

Your search for wisdom and knowledge must begin with God, and then you can transition your search to your earthly brother. God tells us in James 1:5–6, "If any of you lack wisdom, let him ask of God that giveth to all men liberally and unbraidth not; and it shall be given him, But let him ask in faith, no wavering. For he that wavereth is like a wave of the sea driven with the wind and tossed." Start your growth with God with the understanding that by having faith as little as a mustard seed God will strengthen your knowledge, wisdom, and discernment, subsequently allowing you to return the favor to others by you strengthening their knowledge, wisdom, and discernment. When we share our gift with someone else, it expedites the spreading of God's message of loving one's brother unconditionally.

I have lived almost a half of a century on this earth, and the majority of my acquired knowledge has been gained from another brother. This is essentially the meaning of this deep proverb, "Iron sharpens iron and one man sharpens another."

Our ability to make someone else great by sharing our learned knowledge is a blessing given to all human beings.

"OUR ABILITY TO MAKE SOMEONE ELSE GREAT BY SHARING OUR LEARNED KNOWLEDGE IS A BLESSING GIVEN TO ALL HUMAN BEINGS."

GREGORY L. DOCTOR

#50/50

Some individuals I know really buck the idea of gaining knowledge from others or even giving knowledge to others. They love to be the smartest people in the room, but their mental filing cabinets do not contain a lot of file folders. They are against opening their ears and closing their mouths.

Listening is such a superior gift and is so underrated. Listening brings much knowledge to the listener, while the talker is unknowingly sharpening his listening audience. You get to choose which parts of the conversation are relevant and which parts are irrelevant. By thoroughly listening you gain a fuller understanding of the talker's point of view, and then you will be able to be selective on what knowledge you impart to him. Listen more and learn more at the same time. This world needs more constructive listeners and less uneducated talkers.

As a child, I was the youngest of all the children and really didn't have a choice but to listen. I was constantly told by my father, "Old Man," close your mouth and open your ears. This was instilled in me as a child, and it is some of the best information my father could have ever given me. Develop your listening skills, and then you will be more equipped to sharpen your brother in a positive way.

In this life there are biological brothers that hate each other for one reason or another, but they claim to love God. This cannot be so, because if you love God you must also love your brother. If you have done something to offend your brother, you must try to make amends somehow. God tells us in 1 John 4:20–21, "If anyone says, 'I Love God,' and hates his brother, he is a liar: for he who does not love his brother whom he has seen cannot love God whom he has not seen, and this commandment we have from him: Whoever loves God must also love his brother." You asked, "Am I my brother's keeper?" and I will always answer, "Yes I Am."

In life, we sometimes ignore our own shortcomings and get fixated on our brother's shortcomings and blindly ridicule them. Matthew 7:3 asks us, "Why do you look at the speck of sawdust in your brother's eye and pay no attention to the plank in your own eye." We must always inventory our own faults and try to correct them before focusing on fixing other's faults. Once you have cleaned and corrected your own situation, you can then become a better keeper of men.

I work daily to acknowledge the faults that I see in myself and to come up with answers to those faults in order that one day I can be that brother who keeps my brothers while not being a hypocrite to myself. This should be all men's mission in life: to become a better keeper to your brother.

CHAPTER 5

America's Spoiled Soil

To acquit the wicked and condemn the righteous,
both are abominable in the Lord's sight.

—Proverbs 17:15–16

n the year 1619 in Jamestown, Virginia, twenty slaves entered
uncharted territory, figuratively and literally. They were kidnapped from their indigenous land of Africa, shackled, beaten,
some murdered, and subsequently shipped thousands of miles over-

seas to a land, unknown to them, called America. The evil men who perpetrated these inhumane acts set a precedent for exploitation for the next 240 plus years by text, but perpetually by reality. This precedent has affected an entire race. It has become more evident today, in a different and more sophisticated form.

This injustice was created by the devil and will eventually be condemned by God, because whatever you may think in your mind, slavery is not over. Slavery is more prevalent today than ever before; it is just in the form of a chameleon that is ever changing, a hidden bias inscribed within laws and subconsciously in our human minds. Slavery has damaged not only the "African Americans'" psyche but also the "European Americans'" psyche. We have been deprived of our true place in history by avaricious men. When I say "we," I am speaking about the entire human race. These men have used all demographics within the human race as an excuse to fulfill their materialistic desires, desires that have been culminated through one race's pain and sufferings and another race's misunderstanding and misconceptions of the other's true identity. This pain and sufferings is as lucid as the sun's diurnal rising.

These men, being innately infatuated with acquiring and maintaining power, have damaged any possibility of all classes of people living out the true meaning of Dr. Martin Luther King Jr.'s dream and the true meaning of the Declaration of Independence. One of God's dear creations has been and is continually being exploited in a geographical area that is perceived to be the world's "land of the free" and "home of the brave." I agree with only one part of the aforementioned, and, unfortunately, it is the latter alone. This nation is no doubt "the home of the brave," but I beg to differ that it is truly "the land of the free."

America risks her own people to defend countries thousands of miles overseas for humanitarian, monetary, and various other reasons, but won't stop and do the same for the people who are suffering here. This is so unfortunate. If this continues, it will ultimately be the death of a super power. She will have to answer soon for her past and present humanitarian exploitations. I am reluctant to use "she/her" associated with these injustices, because most of these acts were perpetuated and committed by men not women. These terms are only used by me because most people relate the feminine noun to America. I just wanted to explain my position on using "she" as opposed to using "he."

This disappointing act of hypocrisy will one day be America's downfall, unless acted upon with dignity and tact by the past and present perpetrators. Our current situation is not only by fault of our own; it has been a systematic plan that was implemented centuries ago. This systematic plan still goes on today, but by a hidden agenda. This hidden agenda has been discovered by few and deciphered by others. I am one of those others.

To correct these injustices, first and foremost, blacks must receive a public apology for being deprived of our equal rights and common humanity. This would require a public apology for the many centuries of slavery from all the ancestors of slave holders. As stated before, this is not just limited to blacks in America, but also those other races and people who have been exploited by America's past and present biased laws.

Secondly, we must be afforded the opportunity to receive some sort of economic parity and reparations. This must be allocated to all families of African descent and some white families as well, all who have been directly affected by these avaricious men. Since most of this hatred and slavery evolved from the government of the United States, then most of the reparations should be paid by the US government.

We have ghettos and poverty in America because this is what is wanted by a selected few that refuse to let go of the past. I write today not to hold on to the past, but to bring to light how the past has and still is affecting all human beings, in a most pejorative way. There is no turning back now, America is a totally different America now. It doesn't matter who wants to accept it and who doesn't want to accept it—it is what it is. There are more interracial couples and interracial marriages today than ever before, so the fight is no longer solely about black or white. It is now to the more extreme. It is centered on the rich vs. the poor, the upper class vs. lower class, the haves vs. the have nots, and finally the 1 per centers versus the rest of America. Whatever you may want to call it, I call it an injustice.

This is a lot more in-depth than most citizens realize, both black and white Americans. The 1 per centers are where they are now because of the past, and the 99 per centers are where they are today because of the past. Grant it there are many exceptions to my theory, but for the most part this statement is complete and true.

Let's touch for a moment on the effects of people being enslaved versus people not being enslaved. Ask yourself, If no system was in place to teach my family the financial and social ways of America, how would this affect my performance or the performance of my kids or grandkids? Well, I will tell you how.

African Americans have endured slavery, the separation from their true genealogy story, a plethora of murderous acts, defamation, segregation, and now economic disparity. I truly believe that if an honest system had been implemented to help acclimate slaves to the way of life of freedom and if educational benefits were taught and offered back then, then today many things would be different in our society. Because this was not done—and do not be mistaken, it was not done on purpose—we are where we are today as a race. Even though we are where we are, it is not too late to implement this system, but the only difference is, its implementation must now be done by both the white and the black demographic.

I am forced to ask, When will the pattern of negativity end within our black culture? Unfortunately, I believe it will never end unless acted upon by the very people being exploited. We must act somewhat in pursuant to one of the laws of motion discovered by the great Sir Isaac Newton. The first law of motion states that an object at rest will remain at rest unless acted upon by some outside force. This race has continued to stay at rest, being content with its place in this society. But some conscious minds within the black demographic have realized that this outside force of racism affects them, and this has forced them to act. Unless our struggle is ended from within by our fellow brethren, we will continue down a path of despair. We must join the fight against the forces of evil and refuse to remain content with our unfortunate positions in this society. Continuing to be blind and complacent to all the negative incidences that are happening in America is an injustice to all. We must fight against these injustices to bring about change that will positively affect the entire human race. When I use the word fight, it is used in the contexts as fighting wisely against the misguided political messages, the biased commercials, and the prejudice corporations within the American system. This can be accomplished only by educating our minds through thorough research and continually searching for new ways of prospering all people as a whole.

Yes, there are many successful individuals within the black community that do financially well, but unfortunately these same individuals, more often than not, keep their success selfishly to themselves without trying to uplift the needed communities in deprived areas of America.

Let's talk about the rappers, singers, and many other professionally successful black people who forget about the underprivileged. Yes, these same folk may say, "I got where I am because I applied myself and I did the necessary things to be successful. And if I did it, why can't they do it?" Well we do not know everyone's story, and the outlets that are provided to some may not be afforded to others.

God says to whom much is given much is expected, so let us take this simple adage and apply it in the deprived communities of America. Successful people must understand that by not infusing their knowledge and finances back into the underserved communities of America, they are ultimately killing the black community as a whole— and themselves as well.

I talk pretty much exclusively about the black community throughout this chapter because this is my world. But everything I speak about relates directly to all communities that are underprivileged or that have been impacted by America's spoiled soil.

I would like to talk about most rappers today. Notice I said most, because not all rappers use their lyrics to gloat about their finances and what they have and what others don't. The "others" that they are talking about are almost always people of color. What needs to be understood by these rappers is that this type of bragging about your finances is an injustice to your entire community. This is especially true if you are on the one hand bragging about how much money you have and on the other hand rapping about the neighborhood you are from, and in this neighborhood 99 percent of the residence are poor, undereducated, and misrepresented. If you have so much money, how about trying to take some of that money and infuse it into the very neighborhood that you claim? If we get just half of the most successful rappers to apply this simple practice throughout America, it will start the turn of poverty into prosperity.

This theory applies not only to rappers but to all successful individuals in America's capitalistic society. We have to start thinking and applying the team concept to the black community as a whole. So don't be twisted by your short-term riches, because if a plan is not put in place for all, then ultimately the entire black community will continue to be hindered and hurt. We will, as a people, remain at a standstill with only a limited few who can acclaim that they are successful.

If we were to work as a team—especially the wealthy individuals—and share our knowledge along with contributing at minimum 5 percent of our income to some kind of cause to turn around the injustices of the past, then I belief this would create a positive movement forward. This would be beneficial not only for blacks but for the entire human race.

There is no more room for excuses that prevent all individuals from benefiting from the different educational information and references available to us. We must not dwell on the past too much, yet we cannot forget it either, because it will only hinder the progress toward financial parity and social equality. Granted, we must never forget the pain and sufferings that many before us went through in order for us to be this far in the game.

We must understand that no other community will help the black community better than the black community itself. If the black community continues to sit back and depend on the white community to implement new laws and new ordinances that favor them, then the black community will continue to be exploited for several more centuries. Now is the time for incumbent lawmakers who have been able to be a part of the American justice system to use their positions to better equalize the laws of the system for the future of all Americans, not just black Americans. While we must primarily rely on our own resources to escalate progress in the black community, we also should always be open to outside help from all demographic groups of people.

In my opinion, the black community has come further than any other community of people in the history of humankind, considering where we came from and the bias laws, people, and entities that have tried to subdue us. Albeit we have made great strides throughout history, we must now continue to move forward, gracefully. The current boundaries must be crossed with caution and prudence, or else we take the risk of creating an even worst situation for blacks as a whole. We are no longer in the civil rights years. We are now in the informational age, and we must use this for our benefit. Education must stop taking a back seat to materialistic desires and start being placed on our front line of defense for a better place and standing— not only in America but, most importantly, in the world.

We will not and must not try to go in alone to confront prejudices. God created all men equal, and until this fact is permeated throughout America and the entire world, we must not and cannot rest.

Thomas Jefferson wrote in the Declaration of Independence that "A prince, whose character is thus marked by every act which may define a Tyrant, is unfit to be the ruler of a free people." This is a very interesting quote considering its ambivalence to America's political and social environment. Did he intentionally use the words "a free people" because of America's current state at that time? At that time in history, most African Americans were not considered "a free people." Regardless of the reasons he wrote it, I agree thoroughly. But I must ask, who is this prince and how is he related to all of the inequalities of this society? Because most black men in this land are waiting on him to appear and issue out these so-called equal rights and liberties for all. Until he does, this land may be defined as a tyrant. Do not misinterpret my words, because I love this country as much as any other red-blooded American; but truth be told, we have been served an injustice, and this must be express on my part before I leave this earth.

I've served the same country that day in and day out allows black men and black boys to be gunned downed by ordinary citizens and law enforcement agencies and get away with it by justifying it through a biased judicial system.

It is a well-known fact that black lives are taken for alleged crimes of equal or lesser extinct as compared to whites who commit the same type of alleged crimes. The word "alleged" is used intentionally, because most of the citizens who have been negatively impacted by law enforcement are actually shown to be innocent after unexpected videos surface. But still the justice system fails to indict the guilty officers in the bulk of these cases. At this time in human history, we must look past the color of someone's skin or someone's position in society (law enforcement) and look exclusively at the truth in the matter.

CHAPTER 6

A Touch of the Civil War Years

The Civil War was an event that brought to light the effects of war on the human psyche. This war was not just for freedom, but it was a war for honor, pride, justification, and for the future of America. I believe America, at this time in history, was being tested from the almighty.

The nation that enjoyed slavery for so long was now expected to show indifference among all of her people, regardless of skin color. America would not be this strong today in the twenty-first century if it wasn't for this era in history, because America's strength has come from the hands and minds of both black and white citizens.

Why is it that humans have to fight prior to changing toward righteousness? In the year of 1861, America was filled with bloodshed stemming from horrific acts that have tarnished America's history forever. This war was not just a war over freedom, it was a war for human rights; human rights promised to all of God's children.

These human rights—which are still denied, on a broad level, to a select group of individuals—I call "image anatomy." This process takes place when someone automatically forms an opinion of someone else just from their appearance. It may go as far as denying someone their true rights just because of that person's deficiency of looks compared to what the looker expects should be a just look. Instead of viewing God's creation as it should be seen, that being with a neutral lens, some humans automatically view and thus judge humans based on skin color. Blacks went through the struggle of hard labor prior, during, and after the Civil War years, and unfortunately they are still not recognized throughout America and the rest of the world as equal human partners. And yes I said the rest of the world, because racism is by far not just exclusive to America. Yet, it is not exclusive to America, America is where we must start the process of eradication of racism and then the process will spread throughout the rest of the world.

The effect of these struggling times strengthened America's financial system substantially, but unfortunately it disproportionately weakened the black demographic as a whole. Most well-off whites have and continue to enjoy a much easier and simplified lifestyle off the fruits of the labor of past slavery days.

Yet some strong and influential leaders in the black race say it is all low-class black America's fault that they remain stagnate. I don't agree with this type of thinking at all. Yes, we as a people must come together and start planning our way toward freedom from a bias system, and young mothers as well as fathers must be better parental figures for our young kids, but all of this cannot be totally blamed on the way kids are being raised today. The white parental figure must, as well, be better at raising and teaching their children how to be a just and conscious human being for all humans. We must turn it around so the entire human race can *equally* enjoy present-day success from the labors of the past. This process will not be easy.

African Americans have been defined by image anatomy, and this has been based on the color of the Negro's anatomy. Some white men started realizing that this wasn't the Godly thing to do. They realized that it was a time for change, a time for the end of slave labor and the beginning of human advancement. These men wanted to put people and knowledge ahead of slave labor, and they became known as men dedicated to the cause of the abolishment of slavery.

This revolution, as it is known by our society today, would not come without conflict. The conflict came from men with different views and different ways of living. The Confederates, mostly from the South, despised the Northerners for wanting to change a tradition and heritage that thrived in the South. They believed the slavery establishment was supposed to be America's future—a future of slaves serving to the herrenvolk democracy, a future filled with cotton and prosperity for the supposedly supreme race. The abolitionists did not see America's future as such. They did not see a future filled with atrocities, such as hangings and whippings of so-called disobedient slaves. They wanted a change, but there was an extremely high price to pay. They were not only ready to pay this price, but they were determined to pay it with interest.

Men fought for the sake of territories, freedom, honor, and patriotism. Some men fought for their communities, and some fought for their ideologies—Northerners and Southerners who had some of the same core ethics and principles. They served the same God and practiced the same religion. They were so much alike but yet so different when it came to what they pictured America's future to be. The South had prospered from the outpouring of cotton, but the North did not want the expansion of slavery. The North was greatly against this, knowing that if the South acquired new territories, it would make it stronger and America more vulnerable to slavery forever. Slavery forever, could you imagine this evil institution in the year 2018? I can, because it still lives, stronger than ever. It has changed from the cotton fields to the "mind" fields.

The deprivation of education has engulfed most minorities inside a barrel of contentment. Most have become complacent with where we are as a people, which is not far at all, and forgotten what those before us went through to allow us to enjoy the many things we enjoy today. We must remove our blindfolds and begin to heal and excel above and beyond the pains of the past.

CHAPTER 7

What Is History?

History can be defined as a story or record of important events that happened to a person or nation, usually with an explanation of causes and effects. Another definition on record states that it is the known facts about what a person, animal, or thing has done. History, this once unequivocal word, is now being altered to fit any situation.

Let's look very closely at this.

Is it that America has always altered and rewrote her history to cater to certain individuals in her society? I would suffice it to say that America has not only done this, but it has specifically and purposely left out important individuals in its society from her history. She has polished history in order that it shines brightly for certain individuals and not at all for others.

History influences the education system, and the education system influences all and ultimately plays a major role in altering the human psyche. Some postmodern historians are beginning to question historical facts and are investigating where history originated from. Unfortunately, man is the telling agent of history. History always evolves from the mind of the historian; thereby that historian can make certain history more relevant over other history. For that matter, he can eradicate any part of history that he chooses to. He can twist and sway history any direction that suits him or the reader. He controls history but is not a student of history; instead, he's the teacher. If teachers of history have distorted the facts, then our present-day thinking and understanding of this world is shattered. History is then no longer facts, but rather a fallacious narrative from one person's perspective.

Of course, all history is not at risk here, but some history is. Most of America's history has been told through the lens of individuals from prejudice decent. This explains very clearly why most famous African Americans have been left out of essential parts of American history.

Some groups of people, such as the Annales (a group of historians associated with a style of historiography developed by French historians in the twentieth century to stress long-term social history), concentrate their efforts on particular events that are caused by larger currents in the flow of history. They are not concerned about *events*, or so-called historical facts, on which the mainstream focused. Instead, they look at a particular era and investigated how certain events in this era lead to other events.

The Annales were concerned about how functions between the superior social class affected the minority social class. The Annales School implemented more profound studies to establish a better grasp of history by using different social science studies. This group wanted to establish "total history," which I believe is what is needed to establish "true history" in America. A reanalysis of American history is needed in order to reveal "total history" of this nation.

In any history there are things that are incomplete, but American history is not even a tad bite complete. The positive side of American history has been told with biased eyes, and thus they have left out some material facts that would be positively credited to minorities. Some only want the masses to see the negative things of history equated to minorities, but this cannot succeed.

It was not until 1970 that "major" schools cultivated a wider range of historic studies into their system. Women, the oppressed proletariat, and Christians began to receive acknowledgments for the first time in history. History completely turned from the study of major events to the study of marriages, working conditions, and social organizations. The study of the silent masses was implemented. But how could social historians collect data on individuals who never kept official histories of themselves? They went about this by studying symbolic behavior. Studies once again shifted from social history to cultural history, with more attention now focused on language. Some cultural historians now classified history as a "subsystem of linguistic signs." Culture and environment now is the central element of study in history today.

Why is it that these "major" schools did not shift their attention to the less privilege until the 1970s, and why is it that social and cultural history is mainly taught only in major universities? These studies should be embedded into the school system at a much earlier stage.

I bring studying symbolic behavior and "subsystem of linguistic signs" to your attention because social historians cannot recount the true history of a culture solely by studying signs. They must get involve with that people cultures and learn their norms in order to have a true understanding of the indigenous people of that culture. Postmodernists truly have a task ahead of them when they attempt to evaluate which historical facts are more important than others (more importantly, this growing trend of arranging facts to accommodate any situation). In particular, I find Professor Leonard Jeffries's analysis of history very interesting: "Blacks are the 'sun people' while whites are the 'ice people.'" He teaches that all that is warm, communal, and full of hope in history and society has been brought by the sun people, while everything oppressive, cold, and rigid issues from the ice people.

I don't totally agree with his statement, but I understand and feel a sense of interconnection with him. Being someone of African American descent who has been socialized between both ethnic groups, I have experienced most of my love, warmth, and fellowship around blacks. But if looked at differently, I believe that an individual of European descent who has been socialized in American society will probably feel the same toward their people.

CHAPTER 8

The Search for Answers regarding the Economic Disparity between the Races

America the beautiful is worldly renowned for its freedom and opportunity. The land was once defined by chains that shackled the feet of African Americans. These shackles have been removed from the feet of African Americans, but now they have been placed on the African American's psyche. This, in turn, has hindered America's mobility toward advancement in this world.

Why is it that African Americans have gone from one state of slavery to another? Is it because we are perceived to be different? But are we actually different at all? Of course we are different by the color of our skin and by our ethos, but were we different with regard to our intellectual ability during the time of feet slavery? I stress the period of feet slavery because it has been well noted that all human beings' mental intellect is determined by different variables in life and is not based on skin color.

The question of our feet slavery days' intellectual ability will always be uncertain, but I truly believe that there was no difference in intellectual abilities between humans during this time either, just a difference in priorities. The priority for African Americans was to be left alone and raise their families peacefully, while the priority for European Americans was to kidnap, murder, rape, and put certain human beings in bondage. African Americans were removed from their homes, and families and were torn apart in order for America to prosper in her kingdom of cotton.

What I will be trying to prove is that African Americans did not have the same opportunities to become socialized or educated as early as European Americans, so the outcome is our economic standings today, which compared to that of the average European American is substantially less. Hypothetically speaking, let's say that in the seventeenth and eighteenth centuries, when the white man came over to Africa to get slaves in order to labor the fields of America, he decided to go in mutually with everything—for example, labor, productivity, and profits. How about if the African started in the educational system during the same time frame as whites did? How would America be as a country today? There is no doubt in my mind that we would be a much more prosperous America.

Yes, America is the richest country in the world, but we also still have hundreds of homeless and uneducated blacks and whites. My primary interest is in the financial disparity between the two races. Why? It is definitely not a matter of one skin color making one group more intellectual than the other.

Blacks didn't get into the education system until the late nineteenth century. Since then, education, as well as our financial situations, has and continues to increase immensely. This alone is a profound accomplishment. It took many to reach down in the depths of their souls to bring African Americans to where we are today. Individuals who fought so that we could be free today started the process of modernizing our minds in order that we may have a future gain.

I am not prejudiced toward any group of people, regardless of any factor. It helps to remember there were many abolitionists who were at the forefront of the efforts to eradicate hate and slavery, as well as antislavery movements that were also championed by white men. Many laws were passed that hindered white slaveholders, laws such as personal liberty laws that forbade the states from helping slaveholders retrieve slaves who had fled to the Northern free states. These laws were implemented by white men who genuinely wanted to see an end to this great atrocity in human history.

All of these years that Africans were retained as slaves, whites were being educated, so I believe that slavery plays a significant role in why blacks are still behind economically, socially, and statistically in a society that continues to cater toward white America as a whole. Why is it that an entire class of people, which has mutually established this country to the standing that it holds today, still remains financially enslaved and portrayed as inferior? There must be an answer to this, as well as a resolution. One potential answer is that black America has become numb to this very serious problem and has accepted something that is on the same level as slavery. Another answer is that men who do not have our best interest in the forefront of their priorities have created a biased system against us and are fighting to keep this system intact.

One resolution is for us to help educate more individuals, so they become aware of this inferior status that we hold in this society. Once individuals are aware of the subjugation of an entire people, we must then move them to join together to help eradicate this problem.

If we don't get serious about helping ourselves, then certain ramifications will quickly follow. What ramifications am I talking about? Well, if you allow something—anything or anyone—to continue to go in a certain direction for an extended amount of time, then eventually it will take its toll on that entity or person and become as one with them.

Unfortunately, we have unknowingly continued to allow our people as a whole to go on and on with the acceptance of welfare, minimum wage, and average jobs of twelve and thirteen dollars an hour, with the belief that we are actually living the American dream. On a financial comparison between our counterparts, we are making substantially less. This has been the case when it comes to economic parity in the entire existence of America. Ask yourself why and then ask yourself what are you prepared to do as a person to help bring up equality and bring down disparity and ultimately mental slavery in this land called America.

This mental slavery and economic disparity is not exclusive to blacks. It has now worked its way across the board to all races. So even though I speak predominately about blacks in this chapter, avaricious men have no care about what group of people are affected by financial imbalance. They only care about their bank accounts.

It has been shown that the completion of one to five years of college will increase blacks' salaries by 63 percent, compared to 49 percent for a white male (*Journal of Socio-Economics*, Spring, 1994). This information is being presented to illustrate that a good educational background in America will open doors for anyone, not just white males.

Many facts have been presented showing the great disparity in income between black men and white men. But still some will say that they are irrelevant, because other studies—such as this particular one—disclose how black men can close the economic disparity gap. The *Journal of Socio-Economics, Spring, 1994* gathered very interesting facts on the educational enrollment disparity. Some findings consist of the following:

> Between 1973 and 1977 the percentage of black high school male graduates entering college rose from 39% to 48%; by 1983, however, this entry rate had declined to 38%. In contrast, during this same period, the college entry rates among white high school male graduates increased from 48% to 57%.

This study shows that we initially had the right idea, but for some reason we dramatically declined our enrollment. Maybe it was a hidden agenda within the system that worked against blacks once someone saw the increased enrollment statistics, or maybe it was the introduction of a new era in music—that being rap—which was born during these years.

Rap music by far has helped our race beyond imagination, so I am definitely not placing blame on rap for our educational failures. But I am implying that maybe this also affected our race, especially our youth, in areas such as mental growth. And I am not placing blame on the music, I am placing blame on the parents who allowed their child to indulge strictly in this arena and did not place priorities toward the education of their child.

I still can't attribute the lowering of enrollment of young blacks on one single thing, but I can say that whites' enrollment into colleges kept improving while ours declined. Yes, America's system also played a significant role in this declination, but now we must reverse this and get our people back into the education system by any means necessary.

The previously mentioned studies—which show that black men's sala-ries being inferior to that of white men is due mostly to the imbalance in education—gives us the answer to the economic disparity between the two races. That answer is that we must get up and get into the edu-cation system with a vengeance in order to close this gap.

Many will wonder how this can be accomplished, and they will argue the point of not being able to attend college because of inade-quate finances. This is why we as an entire people must start setting up systems to reward our youth as well as our young adults who are hin-dered because of financial restraints. We must establish funds, grants, and programs that are easily accessible for lower- income Americans to start bridging the economic divide. Facts have been presented sig-nificantly supporting both sides of the disparity issue. My opinion on this matter may be a little altered or biased because I am a black man who once competed in America's job market.

I believe that black men are suffering significantly from some type of hidden discrimination that allows only a select few to excel past the masses of white men. This, of course, excludes all types of profes-sional athletes, because society can't limit or discriminate on people's natural God-given talents. There are also some black men who just don't have the motivation to excel; in turn, some disparity in income is directly related to the lack of genuine motivation toward closing this economic gap.

9

Manipulation of America's Biased System

The current system, which was meant to epitomize the constitution, was put in effect for two conspicuous reasons: first, for the uplifting of whites financially, socially, emotionally, and spiritually; secondly, to keep blacks subjugated and "inferior" to whites. These elements have been implemented by prejudice men and championed by even more prejudice men.

Today the prejudice is more inconspicuous than during the antebellum years of the Civil War. These prejudices lie inside the laws and ordinances of America.

Some educated men of today may not even know of the prejudices that are within the American system—or maybe they do—but black America knows well of them. I will refrain from naming individuals, but they consist of the multimillionaire and billionaire groups.

Of course, there are some exceptions, but for the most part these men were aided in their fortunes of today by slavery, which laid a foundation for their fortunes. This foundation grew stronger and stronger over the years, perpetuated through generation after generation, until it exploded into an endless growth of wealth. It is not only a monetary wealth but a wealth of conscious knowledge as well. While they were exercising their minds, blacks were exercising their bodies in the ominous cotton fields of the South. This is very lucid today insomuch as whites are predominantly wealthier than blacks and blacks are predominantly better athletes than whites. This is so because of the exercise of the mind versus the exercise of the body. It is time for us as victims to start exercising our minds to the point of infatuation.

America's present system will remain intact until revised through the efforts of all human beings, yet pushed forward predominated by minorities as a whole. The process must start at home. Parents must start by socializing their child to operate with the current system and not against it, no matter how frustrating it becomes. One should be always able to gear themselves to the crowd, whether the crowd is black, white, Puerto Rican, or Chinese. The crowd at the present time in America is white, so one must learn to operate proficiently within this system.

This socialization is not "selling out" your people, but instead it is helping them. Learning to operate in all realms and entities of life will assist in the liberation of all disadvantaged individuals from economic despair.

I offer many suggestions, but only you can make the proper determination for your current situation. These suggestions will most likely be read by parents of the black youth of today, but you and you alone are responsible for passing them on to your children and other deprived children as well.

First and foremost is advocating for the education of the mind. If America's educational system is unattainable because of financial reasons or biased college entry exams, try a different route.

Exercise the mind diurnally by reading anything you can get your hands on. With this profusion of reading will come a plethora of new words, thoughts, and creative ideas to allow you to escape your current pejorative situation. Look up unfamiliar words, and begin studying a few every day. If you don't own a computer or a dictionary, save to purchase one. Become infatuated with words, and your infatuation will transform your mind. Once your mind is transformed, your finances will follow. America judges you by your use of words and the way one communicates. This judgment is done by both black America and white America. Black America has predominately become acclimated to hard labor through the years of slavery and post slavery. We must change our thought process to correlate with the informational age. Technology is advancing, while minorities are remaining at a standstill or, even worse, going backward. Sadly, some are content with small hourly wages and fifty-plus hours worked every week. We must stop thinking small and start thinking toward owning real state, owning businesses, and advancing our education by any means necessary.

If money is not readily available, I recommend joining the military for two years in order to receive money toward your educational endeavors. If you cannot get behind the idea of putting your life on the line for a country that is prejudice toward your needs, then join the Reserves part-time for tuition assistance solely. This move will be greatly rewarding in the end, and it will help make significant strides toward accomplishing your future goals. The reward of years of beneficial assistance should definitely outweigh the risk of a two- year sacrifice out of one's life.

Today's system has continually brought down to a standstill not only blacks but all minorities. As human beings, we must come together and find new ways to increase our income, as well as our thought processes. You will hear me refer many times throughout this book about elevating our thought processes, because this is a must if we are ever going to become a formidable challenge to the masses of this society. If we remain in an idle state, constantly hoping that our situation will one day turn in a better direction, then we will be waiting centuries for this to unfold.

As stated in chapter 5, Newton's first law of motion states that an object at rest will remain at rest unless acted upon by some outside force. This law is not only true in physics, aviation, and many other disciplines, but it is true in life as a whole. If you are at rest right now in your present life, act to change or you will remain at rest for many years to come—if not your entire lifetime. If you see someone at rest in their present life, be that outside force and act upon that person in a positive way in order to pull him forward toward a success in life. These actions will ultimately help put all minorities in motion.

CHAPTER

Human Responsibility and Human Guilt

God's sixth commandment: "You shall not murder."

—Exodus 20: 2–17, Deuteronomy 5:6–21

This chapter contains some portions of my writings from one of my final papers in Law 813 at Regent University's School of Law. I wanted to insert it in my book to highlight the importance of human life, no matter what circumstance one is faced with.

Who exactly is responsible for the safe keeping of human beings? Is it God, or is it human beings themselves? Through human responsibility, man has been entrusted to keep his fellow man equal, safe, and accountable; safe from negative or illegal acts from within or from any outside intrusions; and accountable for all his wrongful acts.

God created man and then gave him free will—free will to choose between good and evil as well as right and wrong actions in this earthly world. He equipped man with innate senses to either obey or not to obey his natural laws in his blueprint of life called the Bible. This blueprint directs man in every aspect of his life and can lead one to a divine life by following his words within the book.

One of God's greatest communications to man is the Ten Commandments. The six commandment says that thou shall not murder. This commandment, unlike his other commandments, is unequivocally straightforward, subverting the true follower of God's Law from making this wrong mistake and from any ambiguity of what he actually means. This commandment does not elaborate any further. It does not say that it is okay to murder when one is in a dire state, starving to death, or when it is a choice between your life, your child's life, or someone else's life.

Please understand that I am still specifically talking about "murder" here. What would you do if you were faced with your child being kidnapped by some lunatic and all you had to do to set your child free was murder a random person? But if you did not comply, your child would be murdered. Would you commit the ultimate sin of murder in order to save your child's life while unknowingly losing yours? Here is where you have to understand that our lives are in God's hand and not our own hands. If your child's live is at risk, then it is not up to you to take someone else's life in order to save your child's life; this decision is God's decision. Everything else is left to free will and man's interpretation of his immediate situation at the time when he thinks he may or may not need to commit a murderous act. This is the uniqueness of free will; God leaves some of his laws up to open interpretation, and yet in others there is little or no room at all for interpretation.

In this chapter, I would like to explore two resources that reflect on human responsibility and criminal guilt. The first piece, by William Blackstone, discusses the different circumstances surrounding the culpability of a person of a crime under the Common Laws of England at a specific time in history. The second piece is a discussion of a case of cannibalism on the high seas when two men murdered another human being in order to save their own lives.

Let us first start off with how William Blackstone points out the general rule of the land, "that no person shall be excused from punishment for disobedience to the laws of his country, excepting such as are expressly defined and exempted by the laws themselves" (Jeffrey A. Brauch, *A Higher Law: Readings on the Influence of Christian Thought in Anglo-American Law*, 2nd ed.).

Blackstone moves on to demonstrate what makes a crime a crime, that being there must be both a will and an act. Without one of the two there cannot be a recognizable crime, except in three instances:

> Where there is a defect of understanding. For where there is no discernment, there is no choice; and where there is no choice there can be no act of the will, which is nothing else but a determination of one's choice, to do or to abstain from a particular action: he therefore, that has no understanding, can have no will to guide his conduct. (Brauch, *A Higher Law*)

It seems that a lot of murderers can use this "defect of understanding" to their advantage by declaring that they did not understand what they were doing when they committed their crimes. People who are capable of a crime are also capable of dishonestly stating that they did not understand what they were doing and then play out the role until they have been found innocent.

There are so many variables here, such as how old is the perpetrator when he committed this crime? It took this perpetrator all these years to commit a crime of this nature, and all of the sudden he discovers that he has no understanding of the crime he committed. What made him have understanding not to commit a crime prior to committing such a heinous act? Did something all of the sudden trigger something in him? This is one of the three instances that I feel has a loophole in it for guilty perpetrators of crimes to use as a defense.

> Where there is understanding and will sufficient, residing in the party; but not called forth and exerted at the time of the action done: which is the case of all offences committed by chance or ignorance. Here the will fits neuter; and neither concurs with the act, nor disagrees to it. (Brauch, *A Higher Law*)

A will neither concurring with the act nor disagreeing with it will automatically bring forth contradictory issues from the beginning of the evaluation, and this possibly is the reason for this exemption fitting in with chance or ignorance.

> "Where the action is constrained by some outward force and violence. Here the will counteracts the deed; and is so far from concurring with, that it loathes and disagrees to, what the man is obliged to perform" (Brauch, *A Higher Law*, pg. 243).

This exemption actually deals with the unwillingness of an individual to commit a crime but who is by some chance forced to commit a crime. Here everything is in disagreement, and the subject involved does deserve the status of exemption in my opinion.

Next under human responsibility and criminal guilt, we move on to a case of a crime committed in a dire situation. I would like to first highlight the problem with what the captain of the ship, Captain

Dudley, and another passenger, Stephens, did on the high seas. They decided to kill one Richard Parker on the twenty-fifth of July 1884, in order to save their own lives.

First, let's examine Natural Law spelled out by God. I specifically call the Ten Commandments of the Old Testament God's "Natural Law," because a lot of scholars today believe that the Old Testament is irrelevant. I believe that the Old Testament is very much relevant, because it was God's first commandments to man. To throw away God's first commandments to man is equivalent to throwing away humankind as a whole. These commandments are the instructions that put the ball of discipline in motion, so I still hold them near and dear to my heart.

So from this Natural Law, God commanded of his creation (man) to obey all the days of his life. I took the time to notate these commandments from two different books within the Bible, in order to show that there is no differentiation among the original commandments between the different books. The first appearance of the Ten Commandments is in Exodus 20: 2–17, and the second is in Deuteronomy 5:6–21.

Here is the Ten Commandments as listed in Exodus 20:2–17:

> I am the LORD your God, who brought you out of the land of Egypt, out of the house of bondage. You shall have no other gods before Me.
>
> You shall not make for yourself a carved image— any likeness of anything that is in heaven above, or that is in the earth beneath, or that is in the water under the earth; you shall not bow down to them nor serve them. For I, the LORD your God, am a jealous God, visiting the iniquity of the fathers upon the children to the third and fourth generations of those who hate Me, but showing

mercy to thousands, to those who love Me and keep My commandments. You shall not take the name of the LORD your God in vain, for the LORD will not hold him guiltless who takes His name in vain.

Remember the Sabbath day, to keep it holy. Six days you shall labor and do all your work, but the seventh day is the Sabbath of the LORD your God. In it you shall do no work: you, nor your son, nor your daughter, nor your male servant, nor your female servant, nor your cattle, nor your stranger who is within your gates. For in six days the LORD made the heavens and the earth, the sea, and all that is in them, and rested the seventh day. Therefore the LORD blessed the Sabbath day and hallowed it.

Honor your father and your mother, that your days may be long upon the land which the LORD your God is giving you.

You shall not murder.

You shall not commit adultery. You shall not steal. You shall not bear false witness against your neighbor.

You shall not covet your neighbor's house; you shall not covet your neighbor's wife, nor his male servant, nor his female servant, nor his ox, nor his donkey, nor anything that is your neighbor's.

Here are the Ten Commandments as listed in Deuteronomy 5:6–21:

I am the LORD your God who brought you out of the land of Egypt, out of the house of bondage. You shall have no other gods before Me.

You shall not make for yourself a carved image— any likeness of anything that is in heaven above, or that is in the earth beneath, or that is in the water under the earth; you shall not bow down to them nor serve them. For I, the LORD your God, am a jealous God, visiting the iniquity of the fathers upon the children to the third and fourth generations of those who hate Me, but showing mercy to thousands, to those who love Me and keep My commandments. You shall not take the name of the LORD your God in vain, for the LORD will not hold him guiltless who takes His name in vain.

Observe the Sabbath day, to keep it holy, as the LORD your God commanded you. Six days you shall labor and do all your work, but the seventh day is the Sabbath of the LORD your God. In it you shall do no work: you, nor your son, nor your daughter, nor your male servant, nor your female servant, nor your ox, nor your donkey, nor any of your cattle, nor your stranger who is within your gates, that your male servant and your female servant may rest as well as you. And remember that you were a slave in the land of Egypt, and the LORD your God brought you out from there by a mighty hand and by an outstretched arm; therefore the LORD your God commanded you to keep the Sabbath day.

Honor your father and your mother, as the LORD your God has commanded you, that your days may be long, and that it may be well with you in the land which the LORD your God is giving you.

You shall not murder.

You shall not commit adultery. You shall not steal.

You shall not bear false witness against your neighbor.

You shall not covet your neighbor's wife; and you shall not desire your neighbor's house, his field, his male servant, his female servant, his ox, his donkey, or anything that is your neighbor's.

So we can easily see and discern from both books that God is straightforward with his sixth commandment. He states this commandment with four words. There is no room for misinterpretation here. He does not give man an exemption to the rule. He simply states that "You shall not murder," and that means that you should not murder, period! It does not mean that you can murder to save your own life.

I would like for the reader to take notice of the distinction between the words murder and kill here. Wikipedia's definition of "murder" is as follows: "*Murder* is the unlawful killing, with malice aforethought, of another human, and generally this premeditated state of mind distinguishes murder from other forms of unlawful homicide (such as manslaughter)." Wikipedia's definition of "kill" is as follows: "*Kill* may refer to the act of causing the death of a living organism. Homicide may be referred to as one human killing another."

These two men were very much in line with the definition of murder. They had malice aforethought; the murder was planned in advance and was going to be done with no regard to one Richard Parker's life. Captain Dudley's rank meant he had a responsibility for the safe keeping of human life, and he failed. With his failure, he invited others to fail with him as well.

Upon further investigation and a just trial, the courts stated the following, "It is therefore our duty to declare that the prisoners' act in this case was willful murder; that the facts as stated in the verdict are no legal justification of the homicide; and to say that, in our unanimous opinion, they are, upon this special verdict, guilty of murder" (Brauch, *A Higher Law*, pg. 259).

I agree with this verdict wholeheartedly, because if this had not been the ruling, it would have set a dangerous precedence. The preservation of human life should always be placed on the highest of all our responsibilities and never left up to man to decide when to end another fellow human being's life; this must be left up to God the Almighty who created all humankind.

Under diminished capacity we have several different defenses that have come up in recent decades. We have defenses based on post-traumatic stress disorder (PTSD) and battered women's syndrome (BWS), along with such strange ones as the black rage defense and the PMS defense. I take all legitimate conditions into consideration as forms of defenses, but it appears that as time goes on there will be a defense for just about anything, and this will ultimately allow crime to go rampant. We must place our responsibility for protecting our fellow human beings above the highest of all our obligations and try to implement new laws to deter individuals from committing crimes. Once this is accomplished, there will not be any reason to continue to come up with new arbitrary defenses to protect criminals.

A criminal is just that, a criminal, and we must start to see them as that, no matter who they are. The sixth commandment does not vary at all, and it does not give leeway for the killing of unarmed citizens of this society, especially black men. If you are a true follower of

Christianity, you should have unequivocally just received and understood my aforementioned sentence. Yes I am pulling your card, because true Christians do not waver based on the color of a person; they stand by their Christian values. I believe the only thing minorities are asking of America today is to stand by your Christian beliefs, regardless of color. A murderer is a murderer, no matter if he is wearing a hood or carrying a badge. When so-called Christians can watch videos of unarmed citizens being shot in the back, shot with their hands up and so on, and then subsequently make up a justification for the murder, then we as humans—but most importantly Christians—have lost the sense of human responsibility.

Let us try to take back our human responsibility by calling murders just what they are, regardless of who has committed this sin. We all must start to clearly understand this injustice and stop making excuses for all of the murders that have taken place by bad cops. I specifically express "bad cops," because this is what they are. I do not, by far, blame the entire law enforcement community for the actions of some racist and misguided cops. I also stress racist, because if we were to take a closer examination of our current problem of a disproportionate amount of cops murdering "human beings," then we would easily see that racism is definitely the case here. More times than not, when we see or are informed of a man being murdered by the police, it is usually a black man being murdered by a white policeman. Why is that? Think about these different scenarios for a moment: Why don't we see the same number of white cops disproportionately murdering white men? Why don't we see white cops handling white woman disrespectfully? Why don't we see black cops murdering black men? Why don't we see black cops handling black or white woman disrespectfully? Interesting right? Even if you don't find it interesting, I definitely do.

We do not have a complete and thorough police problem, but we definitely have a complete and thorough racism problem within the police department that is not and has not been controlled and eradicated. Yes, I will also agree that there are other variables at play, like lack of positive training and personal insecurities of some cops, but I believe that racism is the root of the problem. Once control of the racist environment happens, then the police community can move toward the eradication of the racism from within their walls of justice.

One of our duties as human beings is to take care of our fellow humans, regardless of color. We must start here first in order to bring balance back to all American's lives.

CHAPTER 11

Crystallization

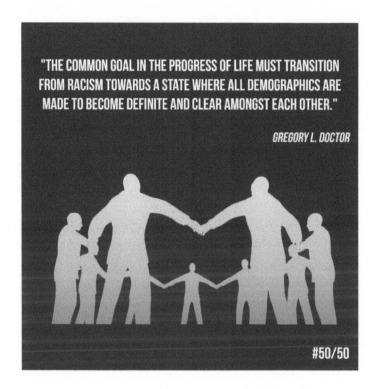

"THE COMMON GOAL IN THE PROGRESS OF LIFE MUST TRANSITION FROM RACISM TOWARDS A STATE WHERE ALL DEMOGRAPHICS ARE MADE TO BECOME DEFINITE AND CLEAR AMONGST EACH OTHER."

GREGORY L. DOCTOR

#50/50

Crystallization can be defined as the process of crystallizing, and crystallizing can be defined as the ability to form crystals or make them become definite and clear. Crystallization must now be brought into the human element of life. The common goal in the progress of life must transition from racism toward a state where all demographics are made to become definite and clear among each other. Let us become crystals, crystals that shine regardless of your skin's pigmentation, your class in society, or your status within this society. We have to move steadfast in the human crystallization journey, because for each step within the crystallizing process there are at least two or three people against crystallizing between the different human demographics. Human crystallizing is essentially the process of seeing past or through the color of someone else's skin color. We must ultimately make the human body become clear as a crystal. When we crystallize, we are able to make further progress toward eradicating racism off of the face of the earth. The human race could then make significant progress in all areas of life, once we are all in the stage of crystallizing.

This process is not restricted to color alone. It can be used to look past all sorts of differences among humans. Being human is not easy, but if I had an opportunity to change, I believe I would decline. We are so unique in our abilities to change the world, but first we must get past our initial shortcomings of visual fixations. Once we are beyond this stage, we will be empowered to do great things.

The human journey is far short of greatness, from a perspective of understanding the universe and understanding each other. I believe that human crystallization can allow us to not only reach other planets, but it will allow us to reach them, understand them, and if desired, inhabit them. This could happen if we bring in more intelligence to the playing field, regardless of skin color, and this can only happen when we crystallize.

Please understand that there are so many intelligent individuals in this world who are being overlooked solely because of their skin pigmentation. The entire world suffers because of this. Crystallize and stop your visual fixation, and watch how fast and far the human race really grows.

Understanding God's entire plan for us as human beings is essential to bringing the human race closer to the process of crystallization. The devil places so many obstacles in our path to prevent this process from taking place, and he has been extremely successful at this since the beginning of time. If allowed, he will control our minds for the next several centuries. But through the process of crystallizing and believing that God is above all, we can achieve greatness and defeat the devil's plan of human destruction.

Life comes and goes, and then we are gone. The process of life then repeats itself with the next set of humans. Hopefully, we all understand that with life comes death and our time on this planet is limited. I am trying to start this process of crystallizing before I leave this earth to be with the Lord, in order that humans can someday be as one, regardless of skin color.

Considering all the other great achievements we have been able to accomplish since the evolution of humankind, I truly believe we can achieve crystallization. This process will not be easy, but it will definitely be rewarding to the entire human race. We must find a way to eradicate any and every type of hate from our hearts. This is not specific to any demographic but instead is required of all human beings. The eradication of hate and racism can happen only by believing in something greater than you and by believing in something greater than your color demography.

I have chosen to believe in God as my something greater, and I am challenging you, the reader, to follow my lead. Through this belief, I have been able to eradicate all types of hatred and racism for any class of people from my being. With my eyes being color blind, I have made better decisions in my business and in life as a whole.

People are people, good is good, evil is evil, and that is what it is. We do not have exclusively black or white crimes, but more precisely we have crime, period. We do not have good white gestures or good black gestures exclusively, but again, we have good human gestures. This is why I wholeheartedly understand that all human beings are equal. Sin and good fluctuates between all, both white and black; we all are cut from the same fabric, and that fabric is God.

Let's take a moment to look at the animal kingdom and learn from them. An ape is an ape, a lion is a lion, a bear is a bear, a wolf is a wolf, a hyena is a hyena—each one of these groups of animals know that they are as one, and they work together as one unit. If you mess with one, the entire group will attack the offender. Why is that? I believe that God has place something innately within the animal kingdom that he wants us to learn from.

To our knowledge, we are the only creatures that have a specific language of communication. This allows us to be on a different level than animals, but it also restricts us. Through language, we can inflict love speech but we can also inflict hate speech. If humans could not speak and were colorblind as it is the case with most animals, everything would have to be based on our immediately interactions between each other. Imagine if we were color-blind and had to define the next man or woman strictly from our encounters with one another. *Wow—*this world would be so different and so special!

This is where crystallization will take you. Allow yourself to start being color-blind. Define people by your interactions and encounters with them, and see how fast and how exponentially God allows you to grow in this thing we call life. Crystallize and be surprised by the human element and not by your predefined misinterpretations of what it really means to be human.

Confusion

Confusion lurks within your mind, heart, and your eyes. Why?

A young intelligent prodigy of society, confused. Confused about life's unknown uncertainties.

Why must life be filled with confusion, and why must you be faced with boundaries that have no limitations?

One is placed in a world to be an elite skilled successor or a poor and ingénue failure of a man or woman; which one will you be?

So, so much uncertainty.

No one really knows if there is reward or macabre horror in the end.

Confusion, will yours ever end?

Will you make it as a man or woman?

Or will you fail to another's reluctant hand? Are you unsure?

Unsure of life, unsure of a wife, unsure of kids, or just plain unsure.

Is it that the cards that you have been dealt are a bad hand?

Relieve your confusion, change your life of illusion, to a life of certainty and eternity.

The life that you want to achieve is always stopped by your adversaries it seems.

They are always sure to see, you say, when you enhance your life in affluent progress. Will they ever rest? I say yes, place your faith in God the Almighty, and your confusion will be laid to rest.

Life is a test, a test that is sure to end. Will you stay confused in this short exam, or will you play God's unchanging hand?

I wanted to start this chapter off with a little inspiration, so that you would understand more about my thoughts on life. We all are placed in this crossword puzzle called life, which, yes, is very confusing, but is nothing but a big troubleshooting problem. If you try different things to achieve the answer to this problem, eventually you will succeed.

Now the question remains, when will one find an answer to life? It depends on how diligently you work toward an answer. Don't take life for granted, because neither you nor I know when that final day will come. As it says in 1 Thessalonians 5, "Now concerning the times and the seasons, brothers, you have no need to have anything written to you. For you yourselves are fully aware that the day of the Lord will come like a thief in the night. While people are saying, 'There is peace and security,' then sudden destruction will come upon them as labor pains come upon a pregnant woman, and they will not escape. But you are not in darkness, brothers, for that day to surprise you like a thief. For you are all children of light, children of the day. We are not of the night or of the darkness that death comes like a theft in the night, you will not know the hour."

With that said, one should work arduously toward making the most out of life and not waste a single moment of it by remaining in the darkness. You must always remain focused on the goals and dreams that you wish to achieve, and one day God will allow all to be manifested.

Patience and faith are the two driving forces behind achieving all of your goals and overcoming confusion. If life was not confusing and everything you desired came to you right when you desired it, you would be like an empty piece of trash floating in the earth's atmosphere. And that alone is even more confusing.

Please understand that every individual is placed on this earth for a very special reason and purpose. It is up to each individual to decipher the material of life until your confusion starts to be minimized more and more so eventually it has been eradicated from your life's challenges completely. As an educated aviator, I understand that the only way an airplane takes flight is by first thrusting against the wind. Through this thrusting against the wind, something special happens at a specific time of ground taxing, and that thing is called flight.

Planes first face challenges before they lift off, and so must humans also face challenges throughout life before God allows us to lift off into free and glorious flight. When you start to believe that challenges and pressures are a part of life and, subsequently, embrace all of those challenges, on that day you will look back and say, "*Wow*, I am actually flying."

CHAPTER 13

The Physical versus the Mental

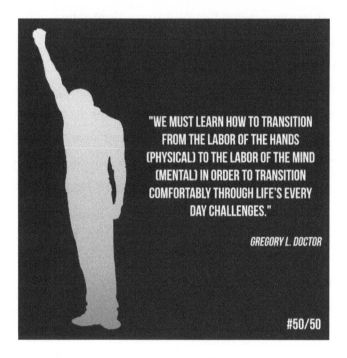

"WE MUST LEARN HOW TO TRANSITION FROM THE LABOR OF THE HANDS (PHYSICAL) TO THE LABOR OF THE MIND (MENTAL) IN ORDER TO TRANSITION COMFORTABLY THROUGH LIFE'S EVERY DAY CHALLENGES."

GREGORY L. DOCTOR

#50/50

The principles of this concept are being explained to help younger generations understand that they can be successful throughout their entire lives by utilizing two tools that God has blessed all human beings with: your mind and your body. Of course, God has blessed us with so much more, but essentially these two are the bases of the hierarchy of all our blessings. When we are born and take our first breath, we are now physically present here on earth and mentally aware of our physical presence. From this point on, we start to grow in both mental and physical states, better equipping us to achieve miracles on this mundane earth. Even though these tools allow everyone to excel, if not used properly, these tools could guide you into a negative life.

With that said, one must understand that everyone involved in a newborn's life, from birth through adulthood, play a vital part in either their growth and development or their underdevelopment and decline into adulthood.

A person's physical growth is almost always dictated predominately by their family's genes, but it can be altered over time to help benefit the individual in sports, physical competition, and many other positive things. I am a firm believer and supporter of the maxim "use what you have to get where you want to be." If one uses this principle, their life will always flow toward where God eventually needs you to be in life.

I believe that everyone is born for a specific reason and is innately tasked by God to find out what the reason is. When people discover for what purpose they were born, I believe it will be the most satisfying moment of their lives; albeit, it will definitely be the most challenging part as well. Some do not ever get the chance to feel this satisfaction, because of the complexity of this arduous task.

Finding who you are and why you are here on earth is, I believe, every human being's requirement once they have entered into this world. It is not to become a doctor, a lawyer, or a millionaire, but ultimately it is to discover why you are here and for what purpose has God granted you the gift of life. To not believe that this is your ultimate goal after entering this thing called life leads to a wasted life here on earth.

Now, to better clarify, if one becomes a doctor, a lawyer, or even a millionaire, this is not a bad thing. It is actually a great thing if it has been done in conjunction with finding your Godly purpose for being here on earth.

Physical strength runs as strong as an ox in our early years and should be exploited to its maximum potential during this time. Our mental strength grows rapidly as well during this time, but it does not fully mature until midlife moving toward our elder years. We must use the mental strength during our early years but especially during our older years, realizing that we will be relying more on our mental strength and less on our physical strength as we age.

We must learn how to transition from the labor of the hands (physical) to the labor of the mind (mental) in order to transition comfortably through life's every day challenges. Both the physical and mental are equally important, but one must know when to implement one over the other. Once this has been learned and mastered, then you are well on your way to becoming a balanced human being.

The 1 percenters are counting on us to stay focused on using our physical strength until we eventually drop dead. You must not honor their wishes. We must, as underserved people of this America, switch the pendulum over to the side of mental exercise and allow it to stay there, regardless of our age.

When you feel this intuition in your soul that you can do great things with your mind, as well as your body, that is the time to switch gears. Switch the gear, and start to accelerate toward greatness.

There is nothing wrong with physical strength, but it is a limiting factor (outside of sports) for your advancement in this capitalistic society. Either learn to gravitate more toward your mental abilities or combine the two forces of mental and physical to achieve greatness. This is what God truly wants for all of his creation. Greatness!

CHAPTER 14

Weakness versus Strength

Who are the weak, and who are the strong? Most men believe that they can determine between the two rather easily shortly after they meet someone. They are right when it comes to ordinary men, but there are a select group of men throughout society who have the capabilities of deception. The loudest person in the room, the tallest person, or the most muscular person in the room are usually *not* the strongest individuals in the room. Sometimes they are, but you cannot be isolated to the visual representation of people and believe that this is what or why this person is strong or weak. People are strong because of their inner being and not, exclusively, because of their outer being.

You must take the time to understand each individual by engaging with them. By engaging thoroughly with someone, you get to know the true person, and then you can balance their inner strength with their outer presence. This will allow you to classify any man—or woman, for that matter—as a strong or weak individual.

But what does it mean, exactly, to be strong or to be weak? I believe that there is no truly strong or weak individual that walks this earth. People are just who God has designed them to be, and that is in his image. God created man in his image, and God is omnipotent, omniscient, omnipresent, and all that. So if all human beings are created in the image of God, then we are all of the above as well. We are not isolated in a class of strong or weak, but since this has been a definitive classification in human society, I shall move forward with the strong or weak discussion.

Deception is more powerful than anyone can imagine. Not that one should go out and try to deceive others purposefully, but when speaking on the subject of what is perceived to be weakness or a strength, one must understand that the two adjectives are actually intertwined.

We all possess both weaknesses and strengths in some form or another. Some may be more evident than others, and some may never be discovered, but one thing that is certain is that they are within all of us.

When I was overseas fighting for this country in Iraq, I sometimes saw little children with book bags or carrying something. As humans, we only saw the children (and the weakness of children). It did not come to light until later that what these children were carrying in those book bags were essentially bombs (strength). We got so fixated on the children and always mistook the situation for weakness, when it was actually a strength situation for the enemy. The power of deception is all around us, but you must always exercise situation awareness of your entire surroundings. After the military started losing enormous numbers of soldiers to suicide bombings of deception, situation awareness training took off.

Someone once said that fear is a powerful thing; they hit it on the head. Fear and fear alone is what awakens our weaknesses. If one can learn to control their fear, then one can also learn how to control their weakness. Once you have control over your weaknesses, your strengths start to blossom naturally.

You see, God made all human beings strong and fearless. Just think back to when you were created and your experiences as a child. Most of us were fearless. God made us fearless, and man made us fearful. Once one understands that fear is only a fallacious creation of man, then one will naturally enter into their Godlike fearless self. Your faith in God and your newly learned knowledge that fear and weakness are elements of man will allow you to release your inner strength out into this world.

CHAPTER 15

Mental Health?

I s it that racism could possibly be linked to mental health issues? One area of study that should be explored is to attempt to trace the root causes of racism, prejudice, and discrimination. Ultimately, we would be investigating if mental disorders/diseases are some root causes to these negative behaviors. I will also be attempting to locate the causes and then identify solutions that will contribute to ending racism. My research will not be exclusive to any one demographically defined group of people, but more specifically, it will attempt to gather information related to all human beings. Albeit I will try and focus on all, my focal point will be more on the history of the effects of racism on marginalized people and how these effects have robbed racial minority groups of success. By providing research on the possibilities of mental disorders being one of the driving forces linked to racism we can uncover deeper understanding of the history of racism. By studying more diverse topics believed to be closely associated with this problem it will give us a broader understanding of the many issues surrounding racism. Moving forward from here, I will attempt to link specific human acts/behavior that I believe mimic behavior associated with the possibility of mental diseases and are contributing factors to the progression of racism.

The need is there to try and identify if any one researcher has been able to link mental disease with acts from the past that may have contributed to increasing racist behaviors and ideologies that pervade our society today, i.e., political radicalization, hatred toward anyone that may look different than you, etc. To discover some type of causal effect, many different topics that are closely associated with one another, to include, but not limited to subjects in psychology, PTSD, youth violence, emotional instability/bi-polarize, spirituality, religion, mental disorders, stereotyping, interracial dating, political radicalization, perceived entitlement, racial profiling and possibly more. There are many dynamics that contribute to racism and discrimination which can cause it to become quite confusing at times, but my essential goal is to somewhat narrow down all these different variables to get a better understanding of why human beings are so active in the aforementioned types of negative behaviors. I believe that once scientist/researchers are finally able to condense all the variables to a more understandable state then we will be that much closer to solving the age-old question of, why racism even exist? If this question is eventually answered correctly then this will bring us closer to finding an effective resolution to this enigma one day. To find an effective resolution, we must first find ways to penetrate the psyche of those perceived human beings who are possibly acting out due to mental disorders/disease in favor of racism and imbalance. With this penetration of the psyche, I believe it can cause the enlightenment of their introspective human soul, which will hopefully allow them to realize once again, or for some for the first time, the value of being a human being. Not until this is understood by all human beings will racism be eradicated. Racism and discrimination have run rampant throughout our entire lifetime and many centuries prior, so either it is a problem that can't be fixed or a problem that the masses do not want to be fix.

There is clear association of racism on the victim's psychological and emotional state, but what caused the perpetrator to choose racism and what mental effects does racism play on his mentality? What drove him to racism? Could he or she have been a victim before? These are still unknowns within the realm of racism, but these are legitimate concerns that need to be addressed to help contribute toward the eradication of racism throughout the world. Could they be suffering from a mental disorder, oppression, or even from PTSD? Holmes, Facemire & Dafonseca (2016) advocate for attempting to add oppression into the PTSD framework as a form of trauma. They note that,

"It should be noted that although expanding Criterion A so that symptoms that follow experiences of oppression could be diagnosed as PTSD is the option predominantly addressed in the current discussion, it is by no means the only way for the field to acknowledge oppression as a form of trauma." (Holmes, Facemire & Dafonseca, 2016)

Furthermore Hall-Clark et al. (2017) study on PTSD relate to "Ethnoracial Differences in PTSD Symptoms and Trauma-Related Cognitions in Treatment-Seeking Active-Duty Military Personnel for PTSD." Because Ethnoracial is such an uncommon word used in today lexicon, I will provide some background on the word. Ethnoracial is associate with both ethnicity and race and the prefix Ethno is also considered to mean race: people: cultural group. Basically, this study searches to differentiate the different affects that PTSD may have on those different ethnicities within the military. They concluded that there is variation in PTSD symptoms amongst the different ethnicities, which I believe can possibility be one of the first steps of many in associating mental trauma, disorders and oppression with post hatred or ease of entry into negative hate groups.

Politics

Moving away from religion and spirituality towards an area in our society that is more prevalent today than ever before, I would like to discuss the realm of today's politics which has contributed to increased racism in American society. Our society has recently accelerated into another dimension that has allowed racism, discrimination, poverty and more to continue to control people's mind. This dimension is the radicalization of politics. It is unfortunate that now if you are a Democrat, you must also be a liberal, pro-choice, pro-black, and so on; and unfortunately, if you are a Republican, you must be pro-police, a racist, pro-life, etc. This is not the order that God has created for his creation to operate efficiently. By placing these divisions amongst man, man himself has put in motion his own demise. As according to McCauley and Moskalenko (2017) Radicalization came to be the word used to refer to the human developments that precede terrorist attack. By evaluating their definition of the word, I believe that most individuals will associate it with groups of people or an act of combined effort. I believe that this word is also linked to the family unit and people, and not just politics. Racist radicalization begins at the birth of a child and is molded into them throughout their younger years by adults and it is not until the unwitting victim of this indoctrination is capable of thinking and processing information own their own, that they either continue with this learned behavior, or turn away from it.

If they choose to abandon it, they now understand the wrong that is intertwined with this type of racist thought process. Let's talk about the Political Radicalization. **Radicalization** can be defined as, the process of making radical.2. the process of becoming radical, (Barnhart & Thorndike, 1978). From here let's define the word Radical. Radical can be defined as both an adjective and as a noun. As an adjective it is defined as 1. Going to the root; fundamental; basic. 2. Favoring extreme changes or reforms; extreme. 3. Having to do with or forming the root of a number or quantity (Barnhart, Thorndike, pg 1719, 1978). As a noun, it can be defined as 1. A person who favors extreme changes or reforms, especially in politics; person with extreme opinions. 2. An atom or group of atoms acting as a unit in chemical reactions. 3. An expression indicating the root of a quantity. 4. Any one of a number of Chinese written characters common to many written words. Out of all these definitions the second definition in the adjective explanation and the first definition in the noun denotation correlates with today's political environment. Albeit McCauley and Moskalenko (2017) study into Political Radicalization is more focused on finding a basis to Terrorism as a whole, I believe that Political Radicalization has now gained a foot-hole into racism and the prejudice nature in America and maybe even throughout the world. In their journal article they are able to associate Political Radicalization with all demographics of people, to include Muslims, people in United States, United Kingdom, Canada, Australia, Spain, and the Netherlands, which tells me that Political Radicalization is not unique to one group of people but moreover specific to all. It can and has been used as a tool to separate and divide people. We must search for prevented measures that will help to eliminate the divide that political radicalization causes in our society. Do positive risk assessment of those that may be on the path of being radicalized but be careful not to misdiagnose an individual's actual position. Sarma (2017) writes, "Effective risk assessment tools need to be able to distinguish between individuals who are on violent and non-violent trajectories. This, in turn, requires a body of research that has isolated indicators that are sensitive to the different processes (assuming they are, in fact, different)". Essentially, the process of evaluation on political radicalization must happen but it must happen carefully. Carefully enough that an innocent individual is not misclassified as a terrorist or as an extremist looking to do harm when they are not on that path.

I believe that religion will one day play a major role in helping to resolve these negative human behavioral patterns. I also believe that the increasing absenteeism of religion, more specifically Christianity, outside of the family unit and outside our school system has been a contributing factor in the increase in hatred and discrimination in America. Because parents have not been adamant about teaching their children about the harm that racism, not only does to the victim, but also to the perpetuator, it has caused excessive damage in human relations. Man must turn his attention from the "love of money" back to "the love of mankind." This about-face will allow God's hand to be more instrumental in where we eventually end up as a people, and when I say as a people, I am speaking about God's creation as a people and not man's creation. Man's creation has put us where we are today; disloyalty amongst one another, hatred for skin colors, racism, economic disparity, inequality, and the lessening of the love for God and his creations.

Those of us that have balance thought towards equality and love for all people must not allow the disproportionate few, dedicated towards division, racism, and imbalanced, to control the narrative of this life. God's plan for man does not align with the harm and dangers that discrimination and racism has brought to humankind and will continue to bring to America and the rest of the world, if it is not harnessed in the wilderness of the neverlands. God tells us that we are all brothers and sisters in this world and must love one another. More specifically, he tells us, "If anyone says, "I Love God," and hates his brother he is a liar; for he who does not love his brother whom he has seen cannot love God whom he has not seen. And this Commandment we have from him; whoever loves God must also love his brother (New Testament, pg. 223, KJV)."

If we as researchers, scientists, and human beings need to solve an existing problem, it is wise to start from the beginning and focus on the root causes of the problem. Racism's roots begin in the times prior to slavery and subsequently floats to the stigmatization of black men by stereotyping them as criminals and violent predators. Is this fair? Most would probable disagree that it is fair, but fair or not, it has been extremely affective to keep one race subservient to another. Najdowski and Bottoms (2015) state that, "There is an abundance of scientific research demonstrating harmful consequences of negative beliefs about Blacks. Particularly relevant for understanding the origins of racial disparities in criminal justice outcomes is the widely documented stereotypes that depict Blacks as violent and prone to crime (see, e.g., Oliver, 2003; Rome, 2004; Welch, 2007. Duru (2004) traced the roots of this stereotype to the 16th century, when European explorers first encountered and enslaved Black men." The fact that this stereotyping of Black Men has been going on since the 16th century and still exist today illustrates that this system is extremely affective and one that man has not implored their full efforts to eradicate it. Maybe it is one that man wants to continue to exist? I will not paint with a wide stroke here, because this system remains not because all men want it to remain, but I believe that it remains because of its effectiveness to subdue marginalized individuals and it allows those that have been in power for so long to keep this power without per se shaking up society. Money and power remain the dominating factors that continue to keep this system alive and well.

Unfortunately, this system has also allowed the killing of unarmed minorities with impunity for both law enforcement and regular citizens. Scientific research cannot pinpoint the causal role of police officers' racial bias-either implicit or explicit-in any one specific shooting incident (Kahn & McMahon, 2015). The key to this inability to pinpoint is that it is aligned with a singular action and based on this reporting does not go to the root of the problem, as well, it does not penetrate the culture of stereotyping that thrives not only in society but more importantly within the majority of America's Police department. The false ideology that all blacks are criminals and violent allows indecent people to kill innocent people at random. This ideology not only puts minorities in danger but everyone in danger, because this behavioral pattern first starts with minorities and eventually transcends to all of humanity. Kahn and McMahon (2015) have also done research which reveals that,

> "Fifteen years of social psychological research has confirmed the existence of shooter bias in nonpolice undergraduate and community samples. This bias results not from explicit racist attitudes but from the unconscious activation of stereotypes linking a particular group to danger, which facilitates stereotypes-consistent responses unless the individual has the cognitive capacity and time to counteract it."

So, as you can see here stereotype has not only affected law enforcement but also regular citizens which essentially materializes into being critically damaging to both the victim and perpetuator.

For centuries many speculated about the possibility of stereotypes on race, especially of the stereotype about the black race and now there is scientific proof that this stereotype behavior does truly exist. As according to Najdowski et al. (2015):

"There is an abundance of scientific research demonstrating harmful consequences of negative beliefs about Blacks. Particularly relevant for understanding the origins of racial disparities in criminal justice outcomes is the widely documented stereotype that depicts Blacks as violent and prone to crime (see, e.g., Oliver, 2003; Rome, 2004; Welch, 2007)."

This negative depiction of Blacks has regrettable plague the law enforcement agencies of America, insomuch that it is not abnormal to see at a minimum of 2-3 shootings of unarmed Black Men within the course of several months, but rarely do we see this trend amongst other demographically groups of people. Most times we see that other racial groups that have committed egregious crimes against mankind are led off to jail unharmed and even treated to Burger King and other favors prior to being processed into jail. Meanwhile, the black minority group are sometimes killed for minor traffic violations. This lies true throughout America, and I am only speaking on it because answers need to be found to fix the problem of stereotyping which subsequently ramps up into the death of someone. The act of stereotyping groups of people will automatically cause behavior changes from that affected body of people when they are encountering, for example, a law enforcement officer on the streets or off a dark desolate road. Moreover, if the law enforcement officer has not had training to understand that groups of people that have been negatively affected from stereotyping may act a certain way because they have actually been innately altered from these bias practices then he may perceive it as suspicious behavior and in turn act aggressively towards the individual. Consequently, Blacks may be more likely than Whites to behave in ways that police commonly perceive as indicative of deception, increasing the likelihood that innocent Blacks will be misclassified as guilty by police (Naidowski, Bottoms, Goff, 2015).

I do find it very interesting that Kahn & McMahon (2015) state that, "To the potential surprise of some, there is a dearth of empirical evidence identifying the causal role of suspect race on police behavior (Goff & Kahn, 2012). That is, little empirical research exists that directly ties police officers' racial attitudes to their behavior with racial minority suspects in the field. Disparity research is prominent, finding differential policing outcomes for minority compared to majority group members (e.g., Ridgeway, 2006). However, disparity rates alone do not necessarily mean that officer racial attitudes were the cause of the disparate outcomes, rather than structural inequalities, biased institutional policies, or the like (for a review, see Goff & Kahn, 2012)."

What makes the analysist interesting is essentially it is deflecting most of the cause and blame of the shooting of blacks and other racial minority groups away from the individual officer and more towards the inequalities that society has instilled upon minorities over time. Meaning this inherit prejudice that emanates throughout our society has also infiltrated our law enforcement agencies that they automatically perceive wrong doings when policing minority groups as opposed to overlooking wrong doings when they are policing majority groups. This means that racism is one root cause of the shooting of unarmed minority groups, although there will be many exceptions relating towards individual prejudices as well as the fact that law enforcement institutions are not being proactive in implementing policies that will deter negative policing. If law enforcement agencies throughout America start to put strict policies in place to stop the shooting of unarmed minorities and the stereotyping nature, I believe that we will see a dramatic decrease in these type shootings. The issue here is that everyone must be onboard and in sync with the training. It can't be based on state law alone but more importantly, it must be a federal mandate with specific timelines and deadlines to complete the training and require certification in minority positive policing for those policing the citizens of America. As stated earlier about the possibility that racism and prejudices act not only affect the victim but also the perpetrator, in Hackney & Glaser's (2013) controlled experiment of racial profiling, it showed that racial profiling may be counterproductive because in most cases it increases the net effect of negative policing of all citizens. There are other research and studies that on their face value appear to be implemented to protect the safety of citizens, but once thoroughly researched the evidence shows differently. These policies are initially aimed at the criminal element in society but in the endpoint evidences appears to show that it hurts us all and is more or less for the financial benefit of others. As according to Cook & Roesh (2011):

> The direction of recent and proposed justice policy in Canada is characterized by more criminal offences and longer periods of incarceration. This policy is based on the rationale that crime in Canada is increasing and the perception that Canadians are not safe. This article reviews whether there is empirical support for the rationale of this policy and the related assumption that this policy will reduce crime and better protect the public. From the existing literature, it seems clear that (1) crime

is not on the increase in Canada, (2) it is likely that the reforms will lower crime rates, and (3) there is a large financial and human cost of the recent and proposed criminal justice policies. We conclude that "tough on crime" policies are not supported by the scientific literature (e.g., Smith, Goggin & Gendreau, 2002; Stalhlskopf, Males, & Macallier, 2010).

This type of practice in police policy is alarming and reminiscent of the policies that then Mayor Ruddy Giuliani implemented in the city of New York in the 1990s that caused the unwarranted increase in racial profiling and harassment of minorities. These are the type of practices that must be eradicated to help move us all towards a more balanced and equal society. This brings to light the concept of what researchers call Emotion-False Memory, which play significant roles in situations as important as convicting an individual and confining him to the criminal system for many years or even decades in some cases. This is another element of the judicial system that must also be examined with a more meticulous lens. Bookbinder & Brainerd (2016) point out that:

> Practical motivations, in particular, have abounded as there are some high-stakes situations in which the consequences of false memories are quite serious (e.g., courtroom testimony, eyewitness identifications of suspects, histories taken during psychotherapy, recounting of battlefield events, histories taken during emergency room treatment, terrorism interrogations). The memories that are retrieved in those circumstances are affect-laden, and hence, one of the most enduring questions

about false memory is how it is influenced by emotional states that accompany past experience.

This is just another area in the law enforcement world that can negatively affect not only marginalized individuals but all humans fighting for their livelihood. An eyewitness can literally be having emotional situations from the past that could possibly allow her to testify falsely when someone's life is on the line. Could this phenomenon of Emotion-False Memory be linked to mental disorders as well? There is no outstanding information to state that it is currently link or not, but it is an area that I believe requires additional research.

Emotion-False Memory could also be linked to stereotyping which may be brought out of an individual when they have been triggered from some past emotional state involving minorities.

This is why I must go back and repeat that any form of racism, prejudice, discrimination or economic disparity is wrong and will eventually affect us all in a most negative manner. Therefore, these elements of life must be eradicated and replaced with the elements of equality and balance. The effects have been proven to cause not only psychological effects, but also physiological effects to the victim. Empirical research has suggested racial discrimination is related to greater symptom levels of mental health outcomes such as depression, suicide, violence, stress disorders, and maladaptive coping strategies like substance use among African Americans (Brown et al., 2000; Carter, 2007; Greene Way, & Pahl, 2006; Polanco-Roman & Miranda, 2013; Sellers & Shelton, 2003) (Hope, Hoggard, and Thomas, 2015).

This is where we must push our profession to provide solid research and evaluation in the field of equality in light of racism. Gill and Corner (2017) state in their study titled, *There and Back Again: The Study of Mental Disorder and Terrorist Involvement:*

> For the past 40 years, researchers studied the relationship between mental disorder and terrorist involvement. The literature developed in 4 paradigms, each of which differs in terms of their empirical evidence, the specific mental disorders studied, and their conceptualizations of terrorist involvement. These paradigms have not, however, witnessed linear and incremental improvements upon 1 another.

I provide this final and well researched journal article's history because amongst the many attempts that I have tried to find journal articles contributing mental disorders to racism, this one journal was the closest. Albeit this journal article relates to mental disorders and terrorist I believe that it is essential information/a starting point in trying to discover if there is a relationship between mental disorders and the culture of racism that forces an individual and groups of individuals to be drawn and eventually trapped into this culture. Some may not be aware that terrorist can be domestic or international, it does not matter the locality because an act of terror is essentially acts of violence conducted on someone else. With that said, I thoroughly associate the noun terrorist to the noun racist, so this article has provided me with essential information on moving even further to discover answers to mental disorders associated with racist acts of terror.

Human behavior can be defined both from a social psychology perspective and from a biblical perspective, but which one holds the most weight is still unknown. Through our studies over the past several semesters in Social Psychology it has underscored the relevance of both disciplines. With that said, I believe we must thoroughly embrace both disciplines if we truly believe.

Hill (2005) states, if indeed God is the author of all truth, as evangelicals are quick to claim, a good Christian epistemology should be open to every legitimate and reliable source of knowledge. I agree with this statement because as a Christian I understand that God is in complete control, and if as an evangelical you have no doubt about him being in charge, you should also understand that God is that power who has allowed for all advancements in psychology and science. And, if we look at this from a scientific viewpoint, you will also agree that science has not been able to solve all the mysteries of the universe, so there must be a higher power than that of science which allows this resolve to go incomplete. That higher power is called God, and if both disciplines were to thoroughly embrace each other, and maintain a mutual respect for one another, I believe we would be able to remove the adage of Living on the Boundary and begin to achieve poignant knowledge of other universes and elevate man more towards the unknowns and closer to God.

CHAPTER 16

Slavery and Racism

For the love of money is the root of all evil: which while some coveted after, they have erred from the faith, and pierced themselves through with many sorrows"

(1 Timothy 6:10 KJV).

The wheels of imbalance have been spinning uncontrollably for a very long time now without significant action to correct deficiencies that are evident between the different racial groups. Now, many woke individuals are attempting to bring the injustices of racism, the unfairness of economic disparity, the shame of discrimination, and the wrongs of prejudices more into the circle of accountability. By identifying the different areas within our life's experience it will eventually create balance amongst all people inhibiting God's earth.

I would like to delve into the negative effects of institutional and systemic racism that are still in place around the world and used as tools that allow the gap of failure and success to widen between minorities and those in the majority class. Moreover, I would like to highlight critical areas that need to be focused on more and for a call to action to be implemented in these areas within America's so called walls of justice in order that one day institutional racism and systemic racism can be eradicated. In addition to that I hope that one day we can lower the high rate of police shootings of African American men and to balance out laws which continue to remain in place today and are in direct correlation to the economic disparities between the races. I will also focus on the negative domino effect of colonialism, which was ushered in many centuries ago, and remains intact throughout our worldly affairs. The exploration of colonialism and slavery evolved centuries ago, and it baffles me on how it still rules today. Albeit its position of control has changed from the fields of America, it has transitioned to the minds of marginalized Americans and accelerated the stagnation on financial growth of a people. Simply stated, it still remains in complete control. In the future, I aim at seeking balance for all people and once the balance is found to immediately implement changes through various research methodologies.

There are specific areas that were once deeply immersed/hidden within the scheme of racism which now are more salient now because of the informational age we are in today as compared to that of the past centuries. My hope and dream are to one day find resolutions to these unsolved mysteries encompassing racism. To find the answers to why some people hate, strictly based on the pigmentation of someone else's skin color. A hate that still runs strong today just as it did many centuries ago. A hate that God condemns. If you are of the human race you understand that God created man and in that sense, we all are brothers and sisters and he is our father. What God says in his word, can't be stressed or repeated enough; He says, that anyone who says,

> "I Love God and hates his brother he is a liar; for he
> who does not love his brother whom he has seen
> cannot love God whom he has not seen. And this

commandment we have from him: Whoever loves God must also love his brother" (1 John 4: 20-21 KJV).

This is the word of God, that unfortunately some men have not been able to obey since the beginning of time. All those that believe in the father and hate their fellow man are not walking in alignment with God's written word. No man has seen God, but yet Christians, those that called themselves Evangelist, and all the other denominations in religion claim to love him. If it is true that they do love him, it is also true that they must love all of mankind for whom they have seen. This is where the hole lies that I believe can be filled. Initially by challenging religious leaders in a positive way and forcing their hands to also challenge their own family members and friends whom they know hate others solely based on skin color. They must challenge them to abide by God's written word, that if you love him, you must also love your brother whom he has created. This love cannot be restricted to your biological brothers and sisters but more importantly it must be specific to all of God's creation. As well, we must challenge religious leaders themselves who hate others because they are of a different race. Religion did not just start and neither did racism, these are entities that have been around just as long as humanity. Because religion has been birthed since the beginning of time, I believe it to be essential to correcting most of our problems related to systematic racism around the world.

To do this, we must attempt to find the answers to issues that may have played essential roles in birthing racism. Questions must be answered, (e.g., why did human beings create racism? Why was slavery ever needed? Was everything about slavery wrong? What made slavery so successful? How can religion be more salient in the quest to eradicate racism off the face of the earth?) These are the questions that we must find honest answers to before we can find solid resolutions. Both racism and slavery have hurt humanity and brought division amongst God's creation. This is more significant than individuals understand, and it is required of me to shed light to those that remain in the darkest about this dilemma on how racism and slavery have touched all of humanity in a negative way. Unfortunately, most people do not understand that racism has hurt the white race just as much as it has hurt the black race and as well hurt all other demographical groups of people.

A significant challenge that I believe in and if successful will bring some resolve is to someday have more integrative work implemented in the space of SRW (Spirituality and Religion in the Workplace). This focuses on whether and how spirituality and religion should be expressed in the workplace. The study of SRW has, to date, been relatively free of denominational politics and ideological conflict (Benefiel, Fry, & Geigle, 2014).

I am a strong champion for religion and spirituality to eventually come out from the walls of churches and be scattered methodically throughout all the societies of the world. Not only must it be scattered throughout our cultural areas, but I believe we must be bold enough to scatter it within our workplace. Our laws are currently based on the concept of religion and the state being separated and I believe that this law would be sound and just if all laws in America were genuinely serving all of God's people.

I have long been an advocate for more inclusion of religion and spirituality, not only in schools for our children, but in schools and the workplaces of adults. For our children this would provide with some type of ethical footing to start from especially if it is not provided in their homes or from their family members. I advocate for this inclusion not only in schools but also throughout the work environments around America. Of course, this is a very controversial topic and because the division of church and state it will most likely never come to fruition in America until laws are revamped. The absence of God within our school system has increased crime amongst our children and violence overall in our society. Benefiel et al. (2014) have research about the positive effects of spirituality and religion in the workplace (SRW) which state, "A number of studies using multiple measures have found SRW to positively be related to organizational commitment, job satisfaction, productivity, and other measures of performance." These positive results are based on adult studies but if administered appropriately in schools I believe that it can contribute to lowering youth violence which also contribute to school shootings and other abnormalities that are happening in our younger generations growth environment. A disproportionate amount of violent crime in the United States is committed by 15- to 24-year-olds (Federal Bureau of Investigation, 2013; Bushman et al., 2016).

These years are the most influential in young adult's life and it is during this time that the introduction or the continual education of religion and spirituality can be most productive in our children's lives. Religion, Spirituality, family values, cultural importance, familial bonds, and the presence of love in young adult's lives all correlate with positive growth no matter the demographical identity of the child. Tan (2018) states that, "The most common and frequent explanation for good academic outcomes of Asian American children is Asian family cultural values." This may appear to reflect specifically towards awarding Asians for their cultural values, but this statement was made in support only for the way children are raised and not from where they come from. In fact, it is from a journal article titled, "*Model Minority of a Different Kind? Academic Competence and Behavioral Health of Chinese Children Adopted Into White American Families*" (Tan, 2018). This substantiates the fact that any race of people can thrive if given the same opportunities and equalities as others. This is all that most marginalized groups of people are asking for, they want to at least start out on the same playing field and be afforded the same equal opportunities to either succeed or even fail in America and around the world. Furthermore, Lun & Bond (2013) write that, "Specifically, the relationship between religiosity and life satisfaction was found to be stronger in societies with a higher average level of religiousness, suggesting that person-culture fit enhances the contribution of an individual's religiosity to life satisfaction." If we can consistently as a nation blend religion into our kid's and young adult's life, I believe that our crime problem will dissipate, and violence as a whole will also decrease. The United States is a religious and spiritual nation. Gallup Polls from 1992 to 2012 indicate that 55-59% of Americans say that religion is "very important" in their lives and another 24-29% say that religion is "fairly important in their lives" (Gallop, 2012a, p. 1; Vieten et al., 2013).

Because racial problems are so diverse and widespread throughout the world there it is no way that one can focus on one area and believe that this one area is the cause of or the solution to racism; the hatred of any demographical group of people based on the color of their skin is a disturbed mindset and should be evaluated more to be classified as one having mental health issues. If it is not a mental issue, then

I believe it sways toward man's greed for money or even both. For the love of money is the root of all evil: which while some coveted after, they have erred from the faith, and pierced themselves through with many sorrows" (1 Timothy 6:10 KJV). Those that do not take the time to critically think about what this scripture is saying can falsely start to believe that money is evil, when it is not. The scripture states explicitly that money is the "root" of all evil and not that money itself is evil. Here lies a significant root cause that if you follow the money throughout history, it can be linked to majority of pejorative acts inflicted upon humanity. There is proof that money was the root cause of why colonialism was put in place and why it became so successful from its inception.

> Like Carmichael and Hamilton's analysis of the US, British racism is best understood through the prism of colonial exploitation, political control, and class cleavages. Britain was established in 1707 as a state which already held colonies, with racial hierarchy being a fundamental part of how it governed. Thus, while Britain is not a white settler colony like the US, it has been, since its inception, an imperial state. The violence of exploitation, resource extraction and land dispossession was rationalized by racial hierarchy, as was the social and political power Britain held over colonized populations. The British state, and its institutions, have therefore always used racism to reproduce a racialized imperial order. Framing Black people as essentially violent, deviant and/or criminal means that racism is a fundamental part of the professional

ideology of British policing. Like the US, we can consider racism in Britain to characterize the normal functioning of its institutions, rather than racist outcomes representing an outlier or fault in an otherwise non-racist system which can be rectified by a committee of government experts. However, this crucial detail in the analysis of institutional racism was set to be sidelined in the 1990s, as the British establishment sought to capture and contain the demands of Britain's community-based anti-racist movements (Elliot-Cooper, 2023).

It is here we see that through colonialist's greed for money that they instituted the stigmatization of an entire race of people. This was done to build up their kingdom, and even though money was the essential reason why it was done, money itself did not do any of the evil acts perpetuated on humanity, only man did.

My future research will be based on bringing clarity to this unsettling stigma in America and around the world called racism. Racism is a very broad subject, and many have attempted in the past to solve this mystery. I will do my part in trying to bring resolve to one of man's greatest plights; his search for equality for all. I will be measuring the whys in specific areas within the scheme of racism that I believe are paramount to one day being successful in providing equality to all human beings. Some areas are 1) Why is it that black men are shot more than other demographical groups of people by the police albeit they make up considerably less than 10% of American Society? 2) Why is it that there are overwhelmingly more marginalized individuals and people of color confined to prisons and their prison sentences are disproportionately longer than that of their white counterparts? These two questions are only small inquiries needed within the dynamic of racism that I label as hidden agendas instituted during slavery days and still successfully flourish in keeping marginalized groups of people throughout our worldly society limited to success. The justice system has not really evolved in areas specific to resolving the wrongs of the past, particularly, in the unfair sentencing and discrimination towards the black community especially when relating to black men. Many laymen will automatically assume, and rightfully so, that the unequal numbers between black men being shot by police versus others being shot by the police will either be due to prejudices that lie within the system or because prejudices men of the past have been successful in stigmatizing black men as being overly aggressive or more aggressive than other classes of people. Attitude nor behavior are defined by the color of one's skin, so it cannot be that the attitudes and behaviors of all black men are the same.

If attitudes are predispositions to act favorably or unfavorably, then the attitudes that one has should predict one's behaviors. From the 1930s on, however, studies showed the weak prediction of behavior from attitude (e.g., LaPiere, 1934). This conception escalated in the writings of Wicker (1969), who provided an analysis of 42 studies that produced a low overall attitude-behavior correlation. Over the past several decades, scholars have devoted a great deal of attention to figuring out when attitudes and behaviors are related and when they are not. Research shows that the attitude-behavior relationship depends on the person, the situation, the attitude (e.g., how much knowledge people have about the attitude object), and the measurement match between attitudes and behavior (e.g., are researchers measuring specific attitudes and specific behaviors or specific attitudes but general behaviors; see Ajzen & Fishbein, 1975, 1977; Fabrigar, Petty, Smith, & Crites, 2006; Fazio & Zanna, 1981; Kelman, 1974; Lord, Lepper, & Mackie, 2008; Smith, Terry, & Hogg, 2006). (Fiske et al. 2009 pg. 355).

So, as one can see, both attitude and behavior are based on many different variables, to include the individuals involved and the situation that is going on at that time. More importantly, what we do know is that they are not automatically linked to the racial makeup of an individual and because they are not linked, the notion that this is why people of color are shoot more than others is just ludacris.

Subsequently, I would like to give you some additional background on racism and information about the imbalance in equality it has causes around the world for many centuries now. As according to History.com Editors (2019) American slavery started,

> "On August 20, 1619, "20 and odd" Angolans, kidnapped by the Portuguese, arrive in the British colony of Virginia, and are then bought by English colonists. The arrival of the enslaved Africans in the New World marks a beginning of two and a half centuries of slavery in North America.
>
> Founded at Jamestown in 1607, the Virginia Colony was home to about 700 people by 1619. The first enslaved Africans to arrive in Virginia disembarked at Point Comfort, in what is today known as Fort

Monroe. Most of their names, as well as the exact number who remained at Point Comfort, have been lost to history, but much is known about their journey."

Slavery has been defined as the original sin of this nation and although slavery did not start in America she has been the biggest benefactor from the roots of slavery. Because slavery has been such an essential benefit to America, is why those of color speak on reparations for those that were directly impacted from slavery. Of course, all people were directly impacted by slavery, but some were impacted in a positive way and others were impacted in a negative way. Those that were affected negatively continue to be harmed by its cause today and those that benefited from slavery in the past continue to benefit from it, substantially, today. Again, I advocate that reparations are needed for "all" that were negatively impacted by slavery. This includes any white families or other races that succumbed to this vicious time in world history. The playing field must be balanced out and reconditioned to help all human beings. This has caused a division that could have been null and void right after slavery but instead the following excerpt pretty much explains where we are:

Following the Civil War, Southern Whites were in a position to initiate repair with those formerly enslaved. However, they failed to do so; the opportunity was squandered. The possibility for deepening the bond between fellow Americans went deeply awry. Initial efforts were repelled, and, instead, dominion over African Americans continued through various forms of legal enactments: "slavery by another name" (Blackmon, 2008) The failure by Whites to respond to reparative impulses, despite a period of unmitigated exploitation of those enslaved, indeed illuminates this critical feature of American racism: Throughout post-Civil War history, except for a brief period of Reconstruction, a reciprocal unconscious cooperation between an African American and a White population has been vigorously thwarted (DuBois, 1935/2014; Foner, 2002; Kendi, 2016). To this day, Blacks continue to occupy a subordinate place in a White supremacist racial hierarchy. Despite the end of slavery, Whites retain almost complete freedom to expect of African Americans their complicity in the hierarchical racial order. Though they are in every other respect dominant, Whites continue to possess an emotionally immature relationship to African Americans. In failing to acknowledge or act upon any reparative impulse, Whites refuse to concede their omnipotent and self-centered conception of themselves or to accept an external reality where they do not occupy its voracious center. Notably, they have collectively refused to apologize for the harms committed to their fellow Americans.

Racism, in fact, thrives on this psychological space between Whites and Blacks, first established in the minds of the slave society and, since then, never effectively challenged. The failure to acknowledge past national wrongs has produced instead a collective psychology frozen in time when domination by race was a formal feature of America and when bifurcation of Blacks and Whites, as slave and free, was codified as law of the land. The racial binary, refashioned because of a new post slavery social order in which Blacks were formally free, nonetheless continues to be cast as a natural, inevitable, and permanent feature of American life. The slave society legislated against White care and concern for those enslaved, and, therefore, the social arrangements likely posed less of a moral or psychological challenge to those in control. In post slavery America, the suppression of a reparative impulse toward African Americans, in contrast, necessitated not only new laws of racial domination but also a greatly invigorated racism, with an amplified and elaborated set of justifications preserving racial domination. A more persuasive racism became articulated incorporating the new "race" science spreading throughout the Western world. This racism emphasized as its essential feature the reality of racial difference. In the name of White supremacy and the preservation of a bifurcated nation, racism, implemented within various institutional settings, was energetically deployed; efforts toward racial reconciliation concomitantly were repelled (Prager, 2017).

The aforementioned excerpt goes deep into the divide of blacks and whites and illustrates why one race feels slighted for so many painful memories and events that they still suffer from. One race that has experienced physical, emotional, and psychological pains in the past and continues to remain a victim of them many centuries later. We must do better to first admit to the failures of the past that were inflicted on people of color and subsequently put in place better systems that will help to balance out the imbalance. Answer the important questions. The question of why systematic racism and institutional racism have become so successful? These questions can be answered by simply realizing that those who have the money agree with it and those that don't have the money have become complacent to America's system and thus have normalized its behavior.

Employment of minorities is basically not an issue at all, it is the type of employment that is offered. Most individuals can go out and find a job or even a career and provide the necessary means to support their family. But it is not solely the issue of employment that marginalized individuals are concerned about, but more importantly, it is the limited access to gainful employment. This is where, unfortunately, the line gets drawn in the sand by those in power that distinguishes significant wealth from average wealth. Institutional Racism is deeply embedded in the laws of many countries around the world, and it will be an arduous task to one day overcome it. Institutional Racism as according to Elliot-Cooper (2023),

> Stokely Carmichael (later known as Kwame Ture) and Charles Hamilton coined the term 'institutional racism' in 1967 in their landmark publication *Black Power: the politics of liberation.*[9] Institutional racism is most simply defined as the process through which an institution produces racist outcomes. Writing in the US context, they use

the analogy of the colony to explain how and why these racist outcomes arise. While Black people in 1960s America do not constitute a colony in the literal sense, they argue that the racial hierarchies of colonialism, and the power used to enforce those hierarchies, are applicable to US institutions. The authors critique capitalism in America, which sees Black workers paid less and working under worse conditions than their white counterparts. They analyze the political power wielded by a state that enforces racist laws or neglects the needs of Black communities. These patterns, the authors argue, reflect the racialized exploitation and violence in colonies like Rhodesia and South Africa. Connected to this are the social outcomes of institutional racism – forms of racial oppression – which were also seen in formal colonization. Poor housing conditions and high infant mortality rates are among the forms of state neglect which contribute to, as Ruth Wilson Gilmore would later put it, Black people's vulnerability to premature death.

All the different faces of Racism have one thing in common and that one thing is called death. Being exposed to such hate every day of one's life simply because you look a certain way, brings on many negative variables. Hoggard et al. (2015) found that,

> Racial discrimination negatively impacts cardiac functioning, but few studies examine the more distal cardiac effects of racial discrimination experiences.

The present study examined the momentary and prolonged impact of lab-based intergroup and intragroup racial discrimination on heart rate variability (HRV) and heart rate (HR) in a sample (N = 42) of African American (AA) women across two days. On day one, the women were exposed to simulated racial discrimination from either a European American (EA) or AA confederate in the lab. On day two, the women returned to the lab for additional physiological recording and debriefing. Women insulted by the EA confederate exhibited lower HRV on day one and marginally lower HRV on day two. These women also exhibited marginally higher HR on day two. The HRV and HR effects on day two were not mediated by differences in perseveration about the stressor. The findings indicate that racial discrimination – particularly intergroup racial discrimination – may have both momentary and prolonged effects on cardiac activity in AAs.

As previously mentioned, because of the nature of racism, minorities have been predominately confined to jobs focused on servitude and not gainful employment which leads toward being financially free. As according to Franklin (2022),

Black workers comprise only about 2% of the workforce of Silicon Valley's top 75 firms, a number unchanged since the mid-1990s (Silicon Valley Index [28]). Despite this enduring underrepresentation, scholarship has largely overlooked the experience of Black tech workers, focusing instead on women or Asian workers (e.g. Cech [14]; Shih [42]). In the corporate world, Black workers are found to face alienation, isolation, stigma, bias and blocked paths to advancement (Feagin and Sikes [20]; Jackson, Thoits, and Taylor [25]). However, the literature has said little about the way racial and ethnic boundaries at work might influence Black workers' relationships with co-workers; collegial relationships that necessarily cross ethnic and racial boundaries and are pivotally important for career advancement and trajectories.

The effect of racism is diverse, and this is why we need to find the solutions to the different faces of racism. It affects our marriage, our children, and our livelihood. Trail et al., (2011) wrote,

In light of the associations between race and marital outcomes, and the attention to the relationship between discrimination and racial and ethnic disparities in other domains, it is striking that few researchers have examined the possible role that the experience of discrimination plays in producing disparities in marriage. There is ample reason to believe, however, that the experience of racial discrimination in one domain of life can have implications for other domains. For example, perceived discrimination has been consistently linked to a wide range of negative outcomes such as hypertension (Clark, Anderson, Clark,

& Williams, 1999; Williams & Neighbors, 2001), cardiovascular reactivity (Richman, Bennett, Pek, Siegler, & Williams, 2007), psychological distress (Gibbons, Gerrard, Cleveland, Wills, & Brody, 2004; Williams, Yu, Jackson, & Anderson, 1997), decreased subjective well-being (Jackson et al., 1996), and negative health behaviors (e.g., substance use; Gibbons et al., 2004; Gibbons et al., 2010; see Mays, Cochran, & Barnes, 2007, for a review). Given the documented breadth of the correlates of racial discrimination, this experience seems likely to be associated with marital outcomes as well. Rather than marriage being a safe haven from the effects of discrimination, it seems more plausible that we simply know less about how the experience of discrimination may be associated with marital outcomes.

Their analysis brings in perspective just how harmful racism and discrimination is to those that are affected by it. It negatively impacts our health, our psychological wellbeing and directly correlates with the high percentage rate of divorces amongst African Americans and other marginalized groups of people, not to mention the strain that is introduced to those in interracial marriages. These are the negative effects that are placed on our marriages, but let's examine how it negatively affects our children. Cheeks et al. (2020) tells us that,

Adolescence is an important developmental stage in which to examine the psychological consequences of racial discrimination among African Americans

(Seaton, Gee, Neblett, & Spanierman, 2018; Smith, Sun, & Gordon, 2019). In the Phenomenological Variant of Ecological Systems Theory, Spencer, Dupree, and Hartmann (1997) argue that experiences of racial discrimination are risk factors that produce chronic stress in African American youth's lives and that this race-relevant chronic stress and the way that African American youth cope with it is implicated in their healthy development. There is consistent evidence in the research literature of a link between racial discrimination experiences and psychological outcomes among adolescents (Benner et al., 2018; Priest et al., 2013). Among African American youth, specifically, substantial research links racial discrimination to poorer psychological adjustment, including depressive symptoms, anxiety, anger, perceived stress, and suicide ideation (e.g., English, Lambert, & Ialongo, 2014; Neblett et al., 2008; Seaton, Neblett, Upton, & Hammond, 2011; Smith et al., 2019; Walker et al., 2017).

Furthermore, as according to English (2020) Recent reviews of racial discrimination assessment among adolescents of color have suggested that there is a need for more developmentally-appropriate (e.g., Benner et al., 2018) and contemporaneously-relevant (e.g., Seaton, Gee, Neblett, & Spanierman, 2018) approaches to racial discrimination measurement among Black youth.

We must provide an avenue to bridge this discrimination gap amongst all our youth or we will repeat the negative events in America's history. Being afraid is not an option, we must allow all groups of people to experience all the different cultures that God has created and bring a more inclusive society working together to achieve the same successes in our lifetime.

Racial socialization represents family communications to youth about how to feel and think about their racial group membership and how to understand and cope with discrimination, whereas racial identity is adolescents' crystallization of those messages and other communications about how they think of themselves as a person of color. Positive racial socialization messages may provide adolescents with a mental framework for understanding discrimination experiences and may allow them to cope with negative race-related experiences and develop connected and positive racial identities (Butler-Barnes, 2019).

It is partly because of the aforementioned data I believe that all of these negative combinations placed on minorities marriages and their children, automatically affects their livelihood and entire well-being. No one can change their racial complexity; they are who God created. To be exposed to constant discrimination your entire existence eventually can take its toll on a person eroding the very fabric of their existence. The problem that lies within racism is that it hurts everyone it encounters. It is not a product of God, but a manmade product and unfortunately those that are in power refuse to right this wrong which was created based upon the needs of avaricious men. These wrongs can be traced back centuries and they remain alive and well in our present-day world. Institutional Racism aimed at subjugating some, for the benefit of others, is a system that takes away the lives of innocent men around the world. It takes away those lives both in a literal and figurative sense. All of God's creation is precious and should be treated and respected as such. The system is killing minorities based on laws that were implemented in the days where prejudice men lynched innocent men from trees. We cannot allow the world to continue in this negative direction and think that additional problems will not come to light eventually hurting everyone and not just marginalized people. This is why the problem of racism must be eradicated off the face of the earth, to save mankind from himself. Man created racism and he knows how to completely end racism, but has chosen not to for the betterment of his existence. All it takes is that boldness and sternness remain in place whenever the effort to eradicate racism is challenged. It will be challenged by those that believe others are trying to gain what they have. This is not the case; most underprivileged individuals just want a fair and equal system that will reward all individuals who put in the work. Until men in power change their hearts and take action to change the laws of institutional racism and the ways of systematic racism, we all must continue to join to counter the negative realities of racism.

My purpose remains to one day eradicate the problem of racist practices that has caused our world to be more divided today than it ever has been before. We must remain focused on bringing mankind together again stressing our unavoidable connection based on our lives lived here together on earth. We all are of one creation and should live together here on Earth in harmony for the short life that God has granted us all. Eventually by displacing abundant amounts of love throughout the world we can bring those that hate because the color of someone else's skin color closer to God's word where he commands us to love our brother and our neighbor. Clarity must be brought to those that do not understand how the negative actions of racism and slavery of the past have damaged all of God's creation. My closure will only come when racism is totally eradicated off the face of the earth. I am quite aware of the enormity of this task and understand that all may not happen within my lifetime but by establishing a strong team dedicated to this cause, I believe that one day this can be accomplished.

CHAPTER 17

Police Shootings

In the year 2020 racial politics in Britain experienced two significant, yet contrasting, interventions. The first, the Black Lives Matter protest movements sparked by the police murder of George Floyd in the US, challenged police racism and state power (Elliott-Cooper, 2023). Why is it that this particular murder was so poignant in the movement of the world to try and do the right thing when policing marginalized individuals? It seems it could be from the nature of how he was murdered and the inaction of the murderer's fellow officers to step in to defend this injustice both contributed to this act being more egregious than previous negative acts done by police authorities. This could have been a moment for all of us to witness the true meaning of being human by the officers moving to defend injustice rather than sticking to a so-called blue code. Like other crimes committed unjustifiably upon people of color, it did eventually fade away, but why do we still see the same behavior from those in law enforcement projected on marginalized people after this major movement? It is because the system must be completely overhauled, and stoppage must not take place until systematic racism is universally canceled. Let's look at what was said by Kahn et al., (2015),

"To the potential surprise of some, there is a dearth of empirical evidence identifying the causal role of suspect race on police behavior (Goff & Kahn, 2012). That is, little empirical research exists that directly ties police officers' racial attitudes to their behavior with racial minority suspects in the field. Disparity research is prominent, finding differential policing outcomes for minority compared to majority group members (e.g., Ridgeway, 2006). However, disparity rates alone do not necessarily mean that officer racial attitudes were the cause of the disparate outcomes, rather than structural inequalities, biased institutional policies, or the like (for a review, see Goff & Kahn, 2012). Nor is it possible for researchers to retroactively determine what motivated a particular officer's decision to shoot in any one given situation. What research can aid in is determining the psychological processes through which decisions operate and the factors that can influence the likelihood of mistaken shooting decisions based on race. With this background, we examine what psychological science knows and what needs further research regarding the role of suspect race in shooting decisions."

For the most part, I do agree with their assessment on the causal effects of why police shootings are significantly higher for minority groups of people, but I would like to highlight some areas of indecisiveness that I believe are important. They state, "there is little empirical research that exists that directly ties police officers' racial attitudes to their behavior with racial minority suspects in the field." I believe this statement to be sound and true, but because police incidences are often investigated by the police themselves may result in empirical research lacking supportive information in support of police officers' racial attitudes correlating with their negative actions when dealing with minorities. If more research were done and conducted by an impartial entity, then I believe that the data would change.

They do highlight the importance of systemic racism imbedded within the institutions of the world that contribute to the behavior of those policing us. This is why laws that were enacted back in the slavery days must be revisited and subsequently revamped to correlate with the changing of time and directly be in balance with the equal treatment of all people. The empirical research information definitively shows that it has always been an imbalance when it comes to policing people of color and my future research will be geared towards finding out why. The imbalance must be resolved and according to Statista Research department (2023),

> "Sadly, the trend of fatal police shootings in the United States seems to only be increasing, with a total 529 civilians having been shot, 70 of whom were Black, as of July 13, 2023. In 2022, there were 1,097 fatal police shootings. Additionally, the rate of fatal police shootings among Black Americans was much higher than that for any other ethnicity, standing at 5.8 fatal shootings per million of the population per year between 2015 and May 2023."

As one can see in the subsequent figure there is great disparity as compared per capita of people by race that are shot to death by the police.

Number of people shot to death by the police in the United States from 2017 to 2023, by race

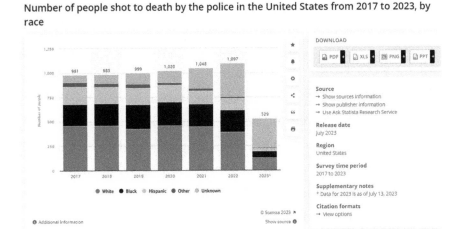

Why is the question; why is this trend repeated consistently every year? A trend that has been repeated for not only decades, but for centuries. I aim at shining a brighter light on the problem of systemic racism that has been allowed to exist all this time and has not been reasonably challenged by those that have the power to overthrow it. Lives are literally being lost because someone in power may be having a bad day and his bad day escalates into taking human life, for offenses as small as traffic violations.

Today's racism is still as powerful as the racism in the 19th century, except today, it is a wolf in sheep's clothing. Racism in the past, meaning slavery time, was bold and in your face, there was no cover up. After this time, it was believed to be neutralized by positive acts like the emancipation proclamation, civil rights laws, and many positive acts by abolitionist; but negative acts such as the black code laws, redlining, and unfair judicial laws aimed at minorities kept it alive and well. People of color continue to be shot unwarranted, imprisoned more, and sentenced to twice the amount of time as other ethnicities that have been convicted of the same crime. This is one of the main reasons that the whys must be answered now, rather than later.

Police corruption is our next face of racism that needs to be uncovered, controlled, or better yet eradicated, is that of police corruption. Police corruption stands at the forefront of racism and contributes significantly to the incarceration of innocent men. The subsequent text sheds light on a case in Miami, Florida about how deep police corruption is embedded into our justice system and into the culture of policing. This type of corruption directly contributes and impacts the lives of marginalized individuals in a major way and is not isolated to the Miami, Florida area but worst off it is nationwide.

> Corruption is a major concern of public agencies, but for law enforcement agencies it is of special concern. Of all criminal justice agencies, the police are the most widely dispersed, readily accessible, and widely visible agents of the criminal justice system (Carter, 1985). Corruption of police officers can arise out of either individual factors or social-structural factors specific to organizational characteristics (Walker, 1983). Delattre's (1989) hypotheses about police corruption include three elements. The first hypothesis involves psychological or individual factors and blames society-at-large, in that citizens provide little gifts and gratuities that can lead to bribes and ultimately to more aggressive criminal activity by police officers. The second is a structural or affiliation hypothesis, which is

similar to the society-at-large model, although it arises from police cynicism based on a loss of faith in humankind; ultimately, corruption becomes acceptable within the department. The third, or rotten-apple hypothesis focuses on the individual officer and the effects of poor recruitment. The rotten-apple explanation is offered by Delattre (1989) as the primary explanation for the River Cops incidents in Miami, although he notes that neither structural nor rotten-apple theories are adequate by themselves nor mutually exclusive (Sechrest & Burns, 1992).

So, as you can see from this article, police corruption is also a diverse problem that must be dealt with and eventually erased from our walls of justice. The police are the first line of defense against corruption in the world and if it is so that did are corrupt themselves, then it only contributes to worsening the walls of justice. I personally advocate for a more thorough selection process when it comes to police recruits. I believe that each recruit should be required to hold or in the process of obtaining a four-year degree in social psychology in order that they be better equipped to deal with the public. Throughout my research on this issue for information supporting higher education for candidate's educational requirements as initial police recruits, I did not find any specific requirements for any four-year degree or associate degrees for new recruits.

CHAPTER 18

Fifty-Fifty Rule of Life

50/50

The fifty-fifty rule of life is used to make the most of our short lives here on earth, in order that we can be well-informed learners the first part of our lives and transition into extremely knowledgeable teachers the latter part of our lives. By blending the two together, we can live a completely balanced life and be in a position to help someone younger than we are live a complete and balanced life much earlier than we did. This system, if taught early on in life, can be a tool to transform the negativity and evil that floats in the atmosphere of our society into smooth, harmonious living for all human beings at all times in their lives.

God promises us three scores plus ten years here on earth, which is the equivalent of seventy years. If we abide by the rules of his lease, our time may be extended. I am an optimist and an analyst of life, and coming from both these points of view, humans are living longer. These days, it is becoming more normal to have a grandmother or a grandfather who is a centenarian. So, I have averaged up to one hundred and split this in half to explain the importance of the fifty-fifty rule of life. Everything in life must be in balance in order to blossom naturally, including the pH balance of life. Without a balance—a fifty-fifty balance, that is—everything is in disarray. Whites and blacks must understand that color does not determine which demographic is more important or relevant than the other. Different Skin Colors have been put within the human element by God to challenge us to cross over this barrier, just as God has placed the different languages within the human element in order for us to cross over that barrier. Starting from the first chapter of this book, "Being Human," I have tried to explain to the reader that being human does not have any labels and is not exclusive to anyone on earth, rather it is specific to all on earth. There is a balance that we must seek in order to live up to our potential, and that balance is fifty-fifty among all human beings regardless of any labels that have been placed on us.

As soon as we are born, the clock begins ticking toward our death sentence. Between birth and death is life. Within the process of life, we should strive for a fifty-fifty balance in order to make our lives all that they are meant to be.

Even though you may find that fifty-fifty balance in your life, just remember that confusion will always accompany our lives throughout the entire journey. Through constant faith in God's plan for your life, your confusion will be balanced out and eventually cemented into certainty. I have frequently been confused throughout my life on what decisions I should make. I've always went with the intuition that God has placed within me. In retrospect, I believe that I have done alright with the decisions I have made.

Make your decision based on the facts that you readily know. If you have suspicious facts but your godly intuition is telling you something, then you must go with the intuition that God has placed within you. Make the decision and then deal with the positive or negative ramifications later, but at least make the decision. Decisions not made are delays in you reaching your goals in life, even if they end up being the wrong decision. A wrong decision can be adjusted to make a better decision, which will lead you to achieve your goals faster. Even though your goals may be harder than they should be, because of the uneven playing field that most minorities deal with, you must continue to move forward. With that said, America must play her part in equalizing the playing field and making fifty-fifty an everyday part of all Americans' lives, not just privileged lives. This is the equality that has been missing from this country since its commencement.

When America decides to be equal in all areas, among all of her citizens, then and only then will she begin the path toward greatness. I am not talking about socializing—capitalism is our way of living and is and has been very successful for us as a nation—but the balance must be equalized to a fifty-fifty baseline.

Seeking a fifty-fifty baseline does not have to be hard for an individual or for a nation; all that is required is for these two entities to become crystallized in their views, be truthful to their Christian beliefs, and to always remember to treat all individuals the way they would want to be treated, regardless of skin color. By crystallizing your views of people and of life, you will find that your immediate situations in life will also start to flourish in a positive direction.

This is what is so great about the fifty-fifty rule of life—you are not only helping others, but essentially you are helping yourself. God wanted balance, and this is why everything takes a fifty-fifty approach. From airplanes seeking the correct weight and balances prior to taking flight, to tape measures in construction having your half measurements between the whole, to God creating balance with our physical beings (e.g., one arm on your left side, one arm on your right side, one leg on your left side, and one leg on your right side). Essentially, our bodies are a fifty-fifty split, and so the universe must follow this or else it will not function right due to imbalance.

America has never functioned correctly, because of the imbalance within it. If a fifty-fifty balance is not implemented, then unfortunately greatness will never be achieved, and the slow deterioration of that entity will eventually eat at its soul until it dies. We all—America as a whole—must incorporate a fifty-fifty balance in our lives, and then greatness will come.

CHAPTER 19

God's Message to You

God has a message for both you and me, challenging us to believe that we have been created in his image and that he loves us more than we can ever imagine. Just think—he allowed us to be created to experience the beauty and glory of life and of earth's natural wonders. What greater gift is there than this—the gift of life?

Really take some time to think about how fragile life is. From our conception until our demise, we are allowed to enjoy his creations, including other humans. There are those who have died before they could be born, those who have died at birth, those who die at an early age, and those who die unexpectedly. They could not read these words of inspiration from God, through me, to you. These individuals did not get the opportunity to experience a full life; they are not privy to the knowledge needed to truly grow with God on this mundane earth.

Have you ever taken the time to really ask, "Why am I still here, and what am I here for?" I have asked myself these questions many times throughout my life. Each time, I then personally thank God for allowing me another day on this earth.

Only God knows what is on the other side after death. Our God has implemented rules and regulations of life through instructions from different books within the Bible. God gives us answers to different variables in life, and he teaches us how to transition to the other side peacefully and gracefully.

Through obedience to his word, we can have anything that our hearts desire. He says ask and ye shall receive, seek and ye shall find, knock and the door shall be opened. It's all right there; he gives us detailed instructions in these short parables.

I recently experienced an unexpected, life-changing event. At the young tender age of forty-six, I suddenly started having excruciating pain in my left ankle. Days later the pain subsided, and I continued to go about my daily activities of working my business and so on. The pain had decreased substantially after a week had passed, but it had now migrated upward.

Running your own business is extremely demanding and challenging, and this was a very challenging time of my life, so I pushed forward without realizing that God was trying to tell me something. I did not immediately listen. A week and some change later, the pain had distinctly migrated from my ankle up to my knee. I was not going to go in to get it examined; as a matter of fact, that was the last thing on my mind, considering the pain was no longer so evident.

I was heading back to the office after a long day working a customer's kitchen ceiling, when something (God) just hit me and spoke to me, saying, "Greg, go to the VA and see what's going on with you."

To make a long story short, my experience at the Veterans Affairs was very challenging and frustrating. The doctor initially wanted to send me home with gout medicine without even doing any x-rays or blood work, but I adamantly spoke up against her verbal diagnosis. The next morning, I had to undergo a peripheral arterial evaluation. It showed that I had a blood clot in the major vein behind my left calf muscle, which could have been fatal. If I had not listened to God and if I had not decided to speak up against the doctor pushing the case of gout, I probably would not be here today. So on a side note, always speak up when it comes to your health if something does not sound right, because it might just save your life. I've always put my fate and faith in God, and he spoke to me that day and spared my life so I could continue to tell his story, which he has placed innately within me. So, I must always deliver his message of love and equality in order that all human beings will become crystallized, and America will one day willingly right the wrongs that have been inflicted on minorities for centuries.

Finally, I would like to tell you that I love you regardless of who you are, regardless of the color of your skin, and definitely regardless of the deficiency of your character! Ignorance is everywhere, but love is color-blind. Let's all decide to spread love and eradicate the ignorance of racism and inequality off the face of this earth together. God bless, and may your life be filled with love, peace, and happiness!

CHAPTER 20

Conclusion

When God create men, he did just that, he created men, not Black men, not White men, not Asian men, not Chinese men, etc. So, from the lens of God, a man is a man and his creation. If God does not allow racism within his Kingdom, then man must not allow it either. I believe that most of all man's problems are birthed from the gift from God, called Free Will. According to Thorndike & Barnhart (1978) Free Will can be defined as, "made or done freely or of one's own accord; voluntary. God has given us Free Will to choose things on our own accord, this includes the opportunity to follow or not follow his teachings of his kingdom, to do right or to do wrong, or to love as he loves, because he essentially has made man of his image (Genesis 1:26 KJV). The notion of Free Will comes into play because humans can practice racism of not practice it, they can choose to love or choose to hate, they can choose to discriminate or choose not to discriminate, they can choose to play fair or choose not to play fair. The choices you make, not only between the aforementioned, but so many other choices in life, will ultimately define you as a human being.

Unfortunately, some in this world have choosen racism and other forms of hate and others have appeared to become immune to it all.

To include the unjustifiable killing of unarmed citizens throughout the world, yet more specifically here in America. They either don't understand or don't care about what it truly means to be human. Outside of this type of moral misbehaving, man chooses to misbehave because of his love for money.

The love of money has contributed to diminishing his innate qualities as relating to human-to-human dignity. Essentially, this love for money (Capitalism and Autocracy) has trumped the recognition of human beings' importance and mutual respect for one another. The elimination of money over the love of humanity must end with the end of racism. The eradication of these stigmas and be extracted from the cultures of all demographical groups of people. The greed of money and racism are not exclusive to the White, Black, Jewish, Asian American, etc., races, but they are dominating amongst all groups of people throughout the world. America ostensibly being the world's leader, must set a poignant example for the eradication of racism and discrimination and not just speak about equality but take immediate corrective actions to implement changes that will result in positive results and rewards for all of her people. These actions must be accompanied with apologies and retributions to all the people that have been negatively impacted by centuries of racism and economic disparities. The American Psychological Association has a great article from October of 2021 titled, *"Apology to People of Color for APA's Role in Promoting, Perpetuating, and Failing to Challenge Racism, Racial Discrimination, and Human Hierarchy in U.S."* While this is not the defining cure for centuries of miscalculated racial practices, it is a great start to healing those that have been psychologically, physically, emotionally and spiritually damaged.

What must be understood by the descendants of the perpetrators of slavery of the past (which has overflowed into injustices of the present) and those individuals that may have sentiments of not needing to apologize because they did not commit these acts, is that they must consider the fact that the system still runs today that was implemented by their ancestors centuries ago and they currently reap the benefits from this system, while minorities continue to suffer from it. Actions must be implemented which allow everyone to have the possibility to reap the benefits of the American system. I use the word possibility on purpose because all minorities are asking for is a chance, not a handout. With a possibility, some will surpass the challenge of accomplishing the American Dream and some will not, but at least all will have increased opportunites to succeed without system limitations because the color of one's skin. The possibilities for rewards can't just be implemented and started today, but more importantly, it must be retroactive to make up for the hundreds of years of economic disparities that have placed so many minorities at a lost and caused great imbalance around the world.

We are no longer in the 19th, 18th, 17th centuries of the past but we have crossed an impasse that has united all people and cultures but unfortunately a fraction of society is trying to control the masses of society by keeping instilled those things that most believe should remain in the past. As according to Mendelsohn, Taylor, et al. (2014):

> Gallop Poll data collected in 1968 showed that 73% of Americans disapproved of interracial marriage, while 20% approved. The percentage of Black respondents approving has been consistently higher than the percentage not approving, but the

percentages moved from 56% approving versus 33% against in 1968 to 85% versus 10% in 2007.

This information is proof of the signs of the time, it illustrates how far we have come as a human race, and we must continue to advance every day to also continue the ameliorating numbers corresponding to racism. The American Psychological Association also has an interested article titled, *Guidelines for Prevention in Psychology.* Within this article it states, "Psychologists are encouraged to conduct preventive programs that have been rigorously evaluated (Guterman, 2004; Weissberg, Kumpfer, & Seligman, 2003)".

ABOUT THE AUTHOR

Gregory L. Doctor is a diverse and unique individual, and he hopes his message will illuminate the blind psyche to conscious, balanced thought. Gregory served in the US Army as a Non-Commissioned Staff Sergeant prior to the events of 9/11 and as a commissioned military intelligence officer post 9/11. Gregory is a 100% Combat Disabled Veteran and has two combat tours of duty with the U.S. Army. He is a Licensed Class A Building contractor, a Licensed Realtor, and he has worked over 30 years in the Aviation industry between the military and civilian sectors. He has Bachelor of Science degrees in both Aviation and Interdisciplinary Studies and holds a Master of Laws Degree in business management from Regent University School of Law in 2017. He is currently working towards a Ph. D. in Psychology and Theology at Liberty University. Gregory currently works daily as the President/CEO of his business Creative Concepts Investments and has enjoyed studying martial arts his entire adult life. He has studied and held belts in Shoran Ru Karate, Kempo Karate, Taekwondo, Kickboxing, and currently holds a purple belt in the martial arts of Hapkido. He is an avid member of his church and loves singing the Gospel.

REFERENCES

American Psychological Association (2021). Apology to People of Color for APA's Role in Promoting, Perpetuating, and Failing to Challenge Racism, Racial Discrimination, and Human Hierarchy in U.S., 1-6

Barnhart C.L., Barnhart R.K. The World Book Dictionary (1978 ed.). Chicago, Illinois: ISBN 0-7166-0278-4

Benefiel, M., Fry, L.W., Geigle, D., (2014). Spirituality and Religion in the Workplace: History, Theory, and Research, 175-184

Bookbinder, S.H., Brainerd C.J., (2016). Emotion and False Memory: The Context-Content Paradox, 1-2

Brown, T.N., Williams, D. R., Jackson, J.S., Neighbors, H.W., Torres, M., Sellers, S. L., & Brown, K.T. (2000). "Being Black and feeling blue": The mental health consequences of racial discrimination. Race and Society, 2, 117-131.

Bushman, B.J. ET AL, (2016). Youth Violence: What We Know and What We Need to Know, 17-21

Butler-Barnes, S. T., Richardson, B. L., Chavous, T. M., & Zhu, J. (2019). The importance of racial socialization: School-Based racial discrimination and racial identity among african american adolescent boys and girls. Journal of Research on Adolescence, 29(2), 432-448.

Carter, R. T. (2007). Racism and psychological and emotional injury recognizing and assessing race-based traumatic stress. Counseling Psychologist, 35, 13–105.

Cheeks, B.L., Chavous, T.M. and Sellers, R.M. (2020), A Daily Examination of African American Adolescents' Racial Discrimination, Parental Racial Socialization, and Psychological Affect. Child Dev, 91: 2123-2140 https://doi.org/10.1111/cdev.13416

Clark-Hall B.H., Zhong J., Asnaani, A., Kaczkurkin, A.N., ET AL., (2017). Ethnoracial

Cook, A.N., Roesch R., (2011). "Tough on Crime" Reforms: What Psychology Has to Say About the Recent and Proposed Justice Policy in Canada, 217-225

Elliott-Cooper, A. (2023). Abolishing institutional racism. Race & Class, 65(1), 100–118.

English, D., Lambert, S. F., Tynes, B. M., Bowleg, L., Zea, M. C., & Howard, L. C. (2020). Daily multidimensional racial discrimination among black U.S. american adolescents. *Journal of Applied Developmental Psychology, 66,* 101068-12.

Fiske, S.T., Gilbert, D.T., Lindzey, G. (2010 Volume One 5th Edition) Published by John Wiley & Sons, Inc. ISBN 978-0-470-13748-2

Franklin, R. C. (2022). Black workers in Silicon Valley: macro and micro boundaries. *Ethnic & Racial Studies, 45*(1), 69–89.

Gill P., Corner, E., (2017). There and Back Again: The Study of Mental Disorder and Terrorist Involvement, 231-241

Greene, M. L., Way, N., & Pahl, K. (2006). Trajectories of perceived adult and peer discrimination among Black, Latino, and Asian American adolescents: Patterns and psychological correlates. Developmental Psychology, 42, 218 –2

Guterman, N. B. (2004). Advancing prevention research on child abuse, youth violence, and domestic violence. Journal of Interpersonal Violence, 19, 29

Hackney, A.A., Glaser, J., (2013). Reverse Deterrence in Racial Profiling: Increased Transgressions by Nonprofiled Whites, 348-353

Hill, P. C. (2005). LIVING ON THE BOUNDARY: SCRIPTURAL AUTHORITY AND PSYCHOLOGY. *Journal of Psychology and Theology, 33*(2), 98-112. https://go.openathens.net/redirector/liberty.edu?url=https://www.proquest.com/scholarly-journals/living-on-boundary-scriptural-authority/docview/223668910/se-2

History.com Editors, (2019). First enslaved Africans arrive in Jamestown, setting the stage for slavery in North America

Hoggard, Lori S et al. "Capturing the Cardiac Effects of Racial Discrimination: Do the Effects 'keep Going'?" International journal of psychophysiology. 97.2 (2015): 163–170. Web.

Holmes, S.C., Facemire, V.C., DaFonseca, A.M., (2016). Expanding Criterion A for Posttraumatic Stress Disorder: Considering the Deleterious Impact of Oppression, 314-320

Hope E.C., Hoggard L.S., (2015). Emerging Into Adulthood in the Face of Racial Discrimination: Physiological, Psychological, and Sociopolitical Consequences for African American Youth, 342-348

Kahn K.B., McMahon J.M., (2015). Shooting Deaths of Unarmed Racial Minorities: Understanding the Role of Racial Stereotypes on Decisions to Shoot, 310-318

Lun Miu-Chi, L., Bond, M.H., (2013) Examining the Relation and Spirituality to Subjective Well-Being Across National Cultures, 304-309

McCauley, C., Moskalenko, S., (2017) Understanding Political Radicalization: The Two-Pyramids Model, 205-216

Mendelsohn G.A., Taylor L.S., Fiore A.T., Cheshire C., (2014). Black/White Dating Online: Interracial Courtship in the 21st Century, 2-9

Najdowski C.J., Bottoms B.L., Goff P.A., (2015). Stereotype Threat and Racial Differences in Citizens' Experiences of Police Encounters, 463-472

New Testament, King James Version (2013) Biblica Direct Service Press, Colorado Springs, CO. ISBN 978-1-56320-793-8, ISBN 978-1-56320-792-1

Prager, J. (2017). Do Black Lives Matter? A Psychoanalytic Exploration of Racism and American Resistance to Reparations. *Political Psychology*, 38(4), 637–651.

Polanco-Roman, L., & Miranda, R. (2013). Culturally related stress, hopelessness, and vulnerability to depressive symptoms and suicidal ideation in emerging adulthood. Behavior Therapy, 44, 75– 87.

Sarma K.M., (2017). Risk Assessment and the Prevention of radicalization from Nonviolence Into Terrorism, 278-288

SECHREST, & BURNS, P. (1992). Police Corruption. Criminal Justice and Behavior., 19(3), 294–313.

Sellers, R. M., & Shelton, J. N. (2003). The role of racial identity in perceived racial discrimination. Journal of Personality and Social Psychology, 84, 1079 –1092.

Statista, (2023). People shot to death by U.S. police 2017-2023, by race

Tan, T.X., (2018). Model Minority of a Different Kid? Academic Competence and Behavorial Health of Chinese Children Adopted Into White American Families, 169-178

Trail, Thomas E et al. "The Costs of Racism for Marriage." Personality & social psychology bulletin. 38.4 (2012): 454–465. Web.

Vieten, C., Scammell, S., Pilato R., Ammondson I., Paragament K.I., Lukoff D., (2013). Spiritual and Religious Competencies for Psychologists, 129-134

Weissberg, R. P., Kumpfer, K. L., & Seligman, M. E. P. (2003). Prevention that works for children and youth: An introduction. American Psychologist, 58, 425– 432.

Milton Keynes UK
Ingram Content Group UK Ltd.
UKHW040717201123
432908UK00002B/454